Identity Security in IoT and Edge Computing

James Relington

DEDICATION

This book is dedicated to all the professionals working tirelessly to secure digital systems and protect organizations from ever-evolving threats. To the cybersecurity teams, IT administrators, and identity management experts who ensure safe and seamless access for users—your work is invaluable. And to my family and friends, whose support and encouragement made this journey possible, thank you.

AKNOWLEDGEMENTS

I would like to express my deepest gratitude to everyone who contributed to the creation of this book. To my colleagues and mentors in the cybersecurity field, your insights and expertise have been invaluable. To the organizations and professionals who shared their experiences and best practices, your contributions have enriched this work. A special thank you to my family and friends for their unwavering support and encouragement throughout this journey. Finally, to the readers, thank you for your interest in identity lifecycle management—may this book help you navigate the evolving landscape of digital security with confidence.

Introduction to Identity Security in IoT and Edge Computing

The rapid expansion of the Internet of Things (IoT) and edge computing has introduced new opportunities and challenges in the realm of cybersecurity. As billions of connected devices generate, process, and transmit vast amounts of data, securing their identities has become a fundamental concern. Unlike traditional IT systems, where identity security is largely confined to human users and enterprise-managed devices, IoT and edge environments demand a more complex approach. Devices in these ecosystems often have limited computational resources, operate in dynamic and distributed networks, and interact autonomously with minimal human intervention. This shift requires a rethinking of identity security to ensure that devices, applications, and users can authenticate, communicate, and exchange data securely.

Identity security in IoT and edge computing involves verifying and managing the digital identities of devices, applications, and users within a distributed ecosystem. Each connected device must possess a unique identity to prevent unauthorized access and ensure secure communication. However, traditional identity and access management (IAM) solutions are often inadequate for IoT and edge scenarios due to scalability issues, lack of centralized control, and the sheer diversity of connected devices. Many IoT devices operate in resource-constrained environments, making it difficult to implement standard authentication mechanisms such as multi-factor authentication or complex cryptographic protocols. The need for lightweight yet robust identity security mechanisms is critical to maintaining trust and resilience in these ecosystems.

A major challenge in securing identities within IoT and edge networks is the heterogeneity of devices. These devices range from industrial sensors and medical implants to smart home appliances and autonomous vehicles. Each device type has its own security requirements, processing capabilities, and communication protocols. Some devices are equipped with secure hardware modules, while others may lack even basic security features. The absence of standardized identity security frameworks further complicates efforts to establish a unified approach. Many IoT deployments rely on proprietary identity solutions that do not integrate well with other systems, leading to fragmentation and increased security risks.

Another critical concern is the dynamic nature of IoT and edge environments. Unlike traditional IT systems, where user identities are relatively stable and controlled within enterprise directories, IoT devices frequently connect and disconnect from networks. Devices may move across different locations, change ownership, or be temporarily offline. This fluidity poses a significant challenge in ensuring continuous identity verification and secure access control. Identity solutions must be capable of adapting to these dynamic conditions without introducing excessive complexity or latency.

Edge computing further complicates identity security by decentralizing data processing and decision-making. In traditional cloud-based architectures, identity verification is often managed by centralized authentication servers. However, in edge environments, computing resources are distributed closer to data sources, reducing reliance on centralized identity providers. While this improves performance and reduces latency, it also creates security gaps. Devices and edge nodes must authenticate each other locally without always relying on cloud-based services. This decentralized nature necessitates innovative identity security models, such as self-sovereign identities, blockchain-based authentication, and distributed ledger technology (DLT). These approaches aim to establish trust without requiring constant communication with centralized servers.

The risks associated with weak identity security in IoT and edge computing are substantial. Compromised device identities can lead to unauthorized access, data breaches, and large-scale cyberattacks. Attackers can exploit poorly secured IoT devices to launch distributed denial-of-service (DDoS) attacks, inject malicious firmware, or exfiltrate sensitive information. Identity spoofing, credential theft, and unauthorized privilege escalation are common threats that must be mitigated through robust security mechanisms. Ensuring strong device authentication, secure credential storage, and continuous identity monitoring are essential steps in reducing these risks.

Identity lifecycle management is another crucial aspect of security in IoT and edge ecosystems. Just as human users have lifecycle stages—onboarding, credential issuance, periodic verification, and deactivation—IoT devices require similar identity management processes. A device's identity must be securely provisioned at manufacturing, registered in an authentication system upon deployment, and regularly updated to reflect changes in ownership or security status. When a device reaches the end of its life, its identity must be properly decommissioned to prevent misuse. The lack of standardized identity lifecycle management often results in orphaned or compromised devices remaining active in networks long after they should have been deactivated.

Interoperability between different identity security frameworks remains a persistent challenge. With IoT ecosystems spanning multiple vendors, industries, and geographic regions, ensuring seamless identity management across diverse platforms is complex. Many enterprises and service providers rely on identity federation techniques to enable secure authentication across multiple systems. However, the implementation of federated identity models in IoT and edge computing is still in its early stages. A universal identity security framework that allows secure and standardized authentication across various devices and networks is necessary to facilitate interoperability and reduce security gaps.

Privacy considerations add another layer of complexity to identity security in IoT and edge computing. Many IoT devices collect and transmit sensitive personal data, raising concerns about user privacy and regulatory compliance. Data protection regulations such as the General Data Protection Regulation (GDPR) and the California Consumer Privacy Act (CCPA) impose strict requirements on how identity information is stored, processed, and shared. Ensuring compliance with these regulations while maintaining efficient identity security mechanisms is a significant challenge for organizations deploying IoT solutions. Implementing privacy-preserving authentication techniques, such as anonymous credentials, zero-knowledge proofs, and differential privacy, can help balance security with user privacy.

As IoT and edge computing continue to evolve, identity security must keep pace with emerging threats and technological advancements. Organizations need to adopt a proactive approach by integrating advanced authentication methods, leveraging AI-driven identity analytics, and implementing zero-trust security models. The future of identity security in IoT will likely involve a shift toward decentralized and autonomous identity management systems that reduce reliance on traditional centralized authentication mechanisms. By addressing the challenges associated with device identity, access control, and trust management, businesses and security professionals can build a more resilient and secure IoT ecosystem.

The Evolution of Identity and Access Management (IAM)

Identity and Access Management (IAM) has undergone significant transformations over the past few decades, evolving in response to technological advancements, cybersecurity threats, and the growing complexity of digital ecosystems. What began as a relatively straightforward process of granting access to local computer systems has expanded into a multifaceted framework that governs identities across cloud environments, mobile devices, IoT ecosystems, and edge computing infrastructures. The need for secure, scalable, and adaptable IAM solutions has never been greater, as organizations strive to balance security, usability, and regulatory compliance.

In the early days of computing, identity and access management were relatively simple. Organizations relied on standalone systems where user authentication was handled through basic credentials such as usernames and passwords. Access control mechanisms were rudimentary, primarily based on local permissions assigned to users by system administrators. The primary focus was on individual workstations or mainframe computers, where identity security was managed in isolation. With limited networking capabilities, identity-related risks were minimal, and organizations did not require sophisticated IAM frameworks. However, as businesses expanded their

13

IT infrastructure, the need for centralized identity management became apparent.

The introduction of networked computing in the 1980s and 1990s revolutionized identity and access management. With the rise of enterprise networks and local area networks (LANs), organizations needed a way to manage user identities across multiple systems and applications. This era saw the emergence of directory services such as Lightweight Directory Access Protocol (LDAP) and Microsoft's Active Directory (AD). These solutions provided centralized repositories for user credentials, enabling organizations to enforce consistent authentication and authorization policies across their networks. While this development improved security and efficiency, identity management was still largely confined to on-premises environments, with minimal concerns about external threats or remote access.

The expansion of the internet and the adoption of web-based applications in the late 1990s and early 2000s brought new challenges to IAM. Organizations began leveraging web applications and cloud services, requiring a shift in identity security models. Single Sign-On (SSO) solutions emerged as a means to streamline authentication across multiple applications while reducing password fatigue. Users could authenticate once and gain access to various services without having to remember multiple credentials. This period also saw the rise of federated identity management, allowing organizations to extend authentication capabilities across different domains and service providers. Technologies such as Security Assertion Markup Language (SAML) and OpenID Connect (OIDC) facilitated secure identity federation, enabling seamless access between business partners and cloud applications.

The rapid growth of cloud computing in the 2010s marked another major shift in IAM. Traditional on-premises identity management solutions struggled to keep up with the demands of cloud-based applications and remote access requirements. Identity as a Service (IDaaS) platforms emerged to provide cloud-native IAM solutions, enabling organizations to manage identities across hybrid and multi-cloud environments. These solutions introduced more advanced authentication mechanisms, such as Multi-Factor Authentication (MFA), adaptive authentication, and biometric authentication. The concept of Zero Trust Security gained traction, emphasizing continuous identity verification and the principle of least privilege. Organizations could no longer rely on perimeter-based security models, as users, applications, and data became more distributed than ever before.

With the proliferation of IoT devices and edge computing, IAM has continued to evolve to address new security challenges. Traditional identity models designed for human users are not sufficient for environments where billions of connected devices operate autonomously. Machine identities have become a critical component of IAM, requiring solutions that can securely provision, authenticate, and manage the identities of IoT devices. Public Key Infrastructure (PKI) and certificate-based authentication have gained prominence as organizations seek secure ways to establish trust in device-to-device communications. The dynamic nature of IoT and edge computing environments also necessitates identity lifecycle management, ensuring that devices can be securely enrolled, updated, and decommissioned when necessary.

The role of artificial intelligence and machine learning in IAM has grown significantly in recent years. Organizations are leveraging AI-driven identity analytics to detect anomalies in user behavior, identify potential insider threats, and automate identity governance. Risk-based authentication systems analyze contextual factors such as location, device type, and usage patterns to determine the appropriate level of access. These intelligent IAM solutions help organizations improve security while minimizing friction for legitimate users. Additionally, decentralized identity models, such as Self-Sovereign Identity (SSI) and blockchain-based identity solutions, are gaining interest as alternatives to traditional centralized identity systems. These approaches aim to give users greater control over their digital identities while reducing reliance on third-party identity providers.

Regulatory and compliance requirements have also played a significant role in shaping the evolution of IAM. Data protection laws such as the General Data Protection Regulation (GDPR) and the California Consumer Privacy Act (CCPA) have imposed strict guidelines on how organizations manage and protect user identities. Compliance with these regulations requires robust IAM frameworks that ensure proper identity verification, data encryption, and access control mechanisms. Industries such as finance, healthcare, and government have specific IAM requirements to protect sensitive data and prevent unauthorized access. The need for strong identity governance and role-based access control (RBAC) has become a standard practice for organizations handling sensitive information.

Looking ahead, IAM will continue to evolve as new technologies and security threats emerge. The integration of identity security with emerging technologies such as quantum computing, 5G networks, and edge AI will shape the next generation of IAM solutions. Organizations will need to adopt more dynamic and adaptive identity management strategies to address the growing complexity of digital ecosystems. The future of IAM will likely involve a combination of cloud-based identity platforms, decentralized identity models, and AI-driven security analytics to provide comprehensive identity security across all environments. By staying ahead of these changes, organizations can ensure that their IAM frameworks remain effective in protecting identities, securing access, and enabling trusted digital interactions.

Unique Challenges of IoT Identity Security

The security of identity in the Internet of Things (IoT) presents unique and complex challenges that distinguish it from traditional identity and access management (IAM) frameworks. The vast number of connected devices, the diversity of device types, the decentralized nature of IoT ecosystems, and the resource constraints of many devices create a security landscape that is difficult to manage. Ensuring the authenticity and integrity of device identities while maintaining scalability and interoperability is a persistent challenge. Unlike human identity security, which typically relies on usernames, passwords, and biometric authentication, IoT identity security must accommodate machine-to-machine (M2M) communication, automated authentication, and secure device lifecycle management. The limitations of many IoT devices exacerbate security risks, requiring new approaches to identity verification and trust management.

One of the most pressing challenges in IoT identity security is the sheer scale of connected devices. Traditional IAM solutions were designed to handle thousands or even millions of users, but IoT deployments often involve billions of devices. Each device requires a unique identity to establish secure communication and prevent unauthorized access. Managing this level of scale demands a highly efficient and automated identity provisioning system. Manually registering and configuring identities for billions of devices is infeasible, necessitating identity automation techniques such as zero-touch provisioning and dynamic identity assignment. However, automating identity provisioning at scale introduces new risks, as attackers may attempt to manipulate the enrollment process to inject malicious devices into trusted networks.

The diversity of IoT devices further complicates identity security. IoT devices range from low-power sensors in industrial automation systems to high-performance computing nodes in smart cities and autonomous vehicles. Each device type has different hardware capabilities, communication protocols, and security requirements. Some devices are equipped with secure elements or Trusted Platform Modules (TPMs) that can store cryptographic keys securely, while others lack even basic encryption capabilities. This diversity makes it challenging to implement a standardized identity security framework that can work across all IoT environments. Many legacy IoT devices were not designed with identity security in mind, leading to situations where devices lack proper authentication mechanisms, making them easy targets for identity spoofing and unauthorized access.

Another major challenge is the decentralized nature of IoT ecosystems. Unlike traditional IT environments where identity management is typically centralized, IoT networks are often highly distributed. Devices interact across different geographical locations, connect to multiple networks, and communicate with various cloud platforms and edge computing nodes. This decentralization makes it difficult to enforce consistent identity security policies. IoT identity security must accommodate devices that frequently change networks, move across different environments, or operate offline for extended periods. Ensuring continuous authentication and secure identity verification in such a dynamic environment is a complex task. Traditional identity federation models struggle to keep up with the fluidity of IoT networks, leading to potential gaps in security coverage.

The lack of standardization in IoT identity security frameworks is another significant hurdle. While there are established identity standards for enterprise IAM, such as OAuth, OpenID Connect, and SAML, IoT devices use a wide variety of proprietary and industry-specific protocols. Different manufacturers implement their own identity management solutions, resulting in fragmented security approaches that are difficult to integrate into a unified security framework. This fragmentation increases the risk of security misconfigurations and weakens interoperability between devices from different vendors. Without widely accepted identity security standards, organizations deploying IoT solutions must invest heavily in custom identity management solutions, which increases complexity and cost.

The constrained resources of many IoT devices further exacerbate identity security challenges. Unlike traditional computing devices, many IoT devices have limited processing power, memory, and battery life. Implementing strong authentication mechanisms such as multi-factor authentication, digital certificates, and cryptographic key storage can be computationally expensive for low-power devices. Many IoT devices lack the capability to perform complex cryptographic operations or securely store identity credentials. As a result, manufacturers sometimes use hardcoded credentials, weak passwords, or insecure identity storage methods, making these devices vulnerable to identity attacks. Attackers can extract hardcoded credentials from device firmware, allowing them to impersonate legitimate devices and gain unauthorized access to networks.

Identity lifecycle management in IoT environments is another significant challenge. Devices go through multiple stages in their lifecycle, from manufacturing and deployment to operation, maintenance, and decommissioning. Each stage presents unique identity security risks. At the manufacturing stage, devices must be securely provisioned with unique identities that cannot be easily forged. During deployment, identity verification mechanisms must ensure that only authorized devices join the network. Throughout a device's operational life, its identity must be monitored and updated as necessary, especially when ownership or network environments change. When a device reaches the end of its life, its identity must be securely decommissioned to prevent reuse by malicious actors. Many IoT deployments lack proper identity lifecycle management, leading to situations where abandoned or outdated devices remain active in networks long after they should have been retired.

The increasing prevalence of identity-based attacks targeting IoT devices further underscores the need for robust identity security mechanisms. Attackers frequently exploit weak authentication mechanisms, identity spoofing, and credential theft to gain control over IoT devices. Botnets such as Mirai have demonstrated how compromised IoT identities can be weaponized to launch large-scale distributed denial-of-service (DDoS) attacks. Attackers can use identity impersonation techniques to inject rogue devices into trusted networks, bypassing traditional security defenses. Without strong identity validation mechanisms, organizations risk having unauthorized devices infiltrate their infrastructure, leading to potential data breaches, system disruptions, and cyber-physical attacks.

To address these challenges, organizations and security professionals must adopt a multi-layered approach to IoT identity security. This includes implementing strong device authentication, using lightweight cryptographic protocols designed for resource-constrained environments, and ensuring continuous identity monitoring. The adoption of emerging identity technologies such as blockchain-based identity verification, decentralized identity models, and AI-driven anomaly detection can help enhance IoT identity security. As IoT ecosystems continue to expand, identity security will remain a critical concern, requiring ongoing innovation and adaptation to address the evolving threat landscape. Organizations must proactively invest in identity security solutions that provide scalability, flexibility, and resilience to protect their IoT deployments from identity-related risks.

Edge Computing and Its Impact on Identity Security

The rise of edge computing has transformed the way data is processed, stored, and managed across distributed networks. Unlike traditional cloud computing, which centralizes processing in large data centers, edge computing brings computation and data storage closer to the source of data generation. This shift has introduced significant benefits, such as reduced latency, improved bandwidth efficiency, and enhanced real-time processing capabilities. However, it has also created new challenges for identity security. As edge devices handle sensitive data and interact with various networks, ensuring robust identity authentication and access control is critical to preventing unauthorized access and identity-based cyber threats.

One of the primary ways edge computing impacts identity security is by decentralizing identity management. Traditional identity security models rely on centralized authentication servers, which verify user and device identities before granting access to resources. In an edge computing environment, however, authentication and authorization processes must often occur at the edge, without relying on a central authority. This decentralization increases the risk of identity breaches, as each edge node becomes a potential attack vector. Edge devices must be capable of verifying identities independently while maintaining secure communication with other network components. This requires strong cryptographic techniques, distributed identity management frameworks, and innovative trust mechanisms to ensure that only legitimate devices and users can access edge resources.

The proliferation of IoT devices in edge computing environments adds another layer of complexity to identity security. Many edge nodes interact with a diverse range of IoT devices, including sensors, cameras, and industrial machines, all of which require unique identities to function securely. Unlike traditional computing devices that rely on usernames and passwords for authentication, IoT devices must use alternative identity verification mechanisms such as digital certificates, public key infrastructure (PKI), and blockchain-based identity management. The challenge lies in securely provisioning, managing, and revoking these identities across large-scale edge networks. Compromised or mismanaged device identities can lead to unauthorized access, data manipulation, and the spread of malicious code across connected systems.

The dynamic nature of edge computing further complicates identity security. Unlike static, centralized IT infrastructures, edge environments are highly distributed and often involve devices that frequently change locations, ownership, or network affiliations. A single edge node may communicate with multiple cloud services, on-premise servers, and other edge devices, making identity verification a constantly evolving challenge. Traditional identity access management (IAM) solutions struggle to keep up with this level of dynamism. Edge computing requires more adaptive identity security approaches that can automatically adjust authentication and access control policies based on real-time context. This includes risk-based authentication, behavioral analytics, and artificial intelligence-driven identity management to detect anomalies and unauthorized activities.

Another significant impact of edge computing on identity security is the increased attack surface. Because edge networks consist of multiple decentralized nodes, each acting as a mini data center, attackers have more potential entry points to exploit. Identity spoofing, credential theft, and privilege escalation attacks are particularly concerning in edge environments. If an attacker gains control over an edge node, they can manipulate identities, impersonate legitimate devices, and gain unauthorized access to critical systems. This makes identity security one of the most crucial aspects of protecting edge deployments from cyber threats. Strong identity authentication, secure key management, and continuous identity monitoring are essential for preventing such attacks.

Data sovereignty and privacy concerns also play a major role in shaping identity security in edge computing. Many organizations deploy edge infrastructure to comply with data localization laws and reduce reliance on external cloud providers. However, storing and processing data at the edge means that sensitive identity information is distributed across multiple locations, increasing the risk of exposure. Unlike centralized identity management systems that enforce strict data access policies within a secure cloud environment, edge computing requires more granular access controls. Role-based access control (RBAC) and attribute-based access control (ABAC) must be implemented at the edge to ensure that only authorized users and devices can access identity-related data. Additionally, encryption techniques such as homomorphic encryption and secure multi-party computation can help protect identity information without compromising processing capabilities.

The integration of artificial intelligence and machine learning in edge computing introduces both opportunities and risks for identity security. AI-driven identity verification can enhance authentication processes by analyzing user behavior, device characteristics, and contextual factors to determine the legitimacy of access requests. Machine learning algorithms can detect identity fraud, identify unauthorized access attempts, and predict potential security threats before they materialize. However, attackers can also leverage AI to bypass identity security mechanisms, generate deepfake biometric credentials, or automate large-scale identity attacks. Edge security frameworks must incorporate advanced AI-driven identity defense mechanisms to stay ahead of evolving threats.

Another challenge in securing identities at the edge is managing identity lifecycles effectively. Just as human users require identity management processes such as onboarding, credential renewal, and deactivation, edge devices and services need structured identity governance. An edge node or IoT device may require identity updates when its firmware is upgraded, when it moves between network zones, or when it changes ownership. Without proper identity lifecycle management, outdated or orphaned identities can become security liabilities. Organizations deploying edge solutions must ensure that identity credentials are regularly updated, rotated, and revoked as needed. Automation tools and identity governance frameworks can help streamline this process while reducing the risk of human error.

Interoperability between different identity security frameworks remains a major challenge in edge computing. Because edge networks often involve multiple vendors, platforms, and cloud providers, identity security must be seamless across different environments. Identity federation techniques enable users and devices to authenticate across multiple domains without needing separate credentials for each service. However, achieving interoperability at the edge requires adherence to open identity standards, such as OAuth, OpenID Connect, and decentralized identity protocols. Many edge deployments still rely on proprietary identity solutions that lack cross-platform compatibility, leading to security gaps and integration difficulties. The future of edge identity security will likely involve greater standardization and the adoption of decentralized identity models that eliminate reliance on centralized authentication providers.

Organizations adopting edge computing must prioritize identity security as a foundational element of their security strategy. By implementing strong authentication methods, decentralizing identity management responsibly, and leveraging AI-driven identity protection, they can reduce the risks associated with identity-based attacks. As edge computing continues to expand across industries, identity security will remain a critical area of focus, influencing how organizations design, deploy, and protect their distributed infrastructures. Adapting to the complexities of identity security in edge environments will be essential for ensuring the resilience and integrity of next-generation computing ecosystems.

Authentication Mechanisms for IoT Devices

Authentication is a fundamental pillar of security in the Internet of Things, ensuring that devices, users, and applications can verify their identities before communicating or exchanging data. Unlike traditional IT systems, where authentication is primarily focused on human users with passwords, multi-factor authentication, or biometrics, IoT authentication must accommodate billions of devices with varying computational capabilities, network environments, and security requirements. The challenge lies in designing authentication mechanisms that are not only secure but also efficient and scalable for the highly diverse and distributed nature of IoT ecosystems. Given that many IoT devices operate autonomously and in remote or resource-constrained environments, traditional authentication approaches must be adapted or replaced with more lightweight and automated methods.

One of the most widely used authentication methods for IoT devices is public key infrastructure (PKI). PKI provides a strong and scalable way to authenticate devices through the use of asymmetric cryptographic keys. Each device is assigned a unique digital certificate, signed by a trusted certificate authority (CA), which proves its identity. When an IoT device attempts to connect to a network or communicate with another device, it presents its certificate, and the recipient verifies its authenticity using the CA's public key. This approach ensures that only authenticated devices can participate in secure communications, reducing the risk of identity spoofing and unauthorized access. However, PKI authentication requires a robust certificate management system, including secure key storage, certificate issuance, renewal, and revocation. Many IoT devices lack the necessary computational power or secure storage to handle PKI operations effectively, making this approach challenging for constrained environments.

Another common authentication mechanism in IoT is pre-shared key (PSK) authentication. In this method, devices are pre-configured with a shared secret key that is used to authenticate them within a trusted network. When a device joins the network, it presents the key, and the network verifies it against a stored database of authorized devices. PSK authentication is lightweight and does not require the complexity of PKI, making it ideal for low-power IoT devices. However, it presents several security risks, particularly if the shared key is hardcoded into firmware or reused across multiple devices. If an attacker compromises one device, they can extract the key and use it to impersonate other devices on the network. Secure key distribution and periodic key rotation are essential to mitigating these risks, but managing these processes at scale remains a challenge.

Device identity authentication can also be achieved through secure hardware-based solutions, such as Trusted Platform Modules (TPMs) or Hardware Security Modules (HSMs). These components provide a secure enclave for storing cryptographic keys and performing authentication operations, protecting device identities from software-based attacks. TPMs and HSMs enable secure boot mechanisms, ensuring that only trusted firmware and software are loaded onto a device at startup. This prevents attackers from injecting malicious code that could manipulate authentication processes. While hardware-based authentication provides strong security guarantees, it increases manufacturing costs and may not be feasible for low-cost IoT devices. Additionally, secure provisioning of device identities during manufacturing must be carefully managed to prevent supply chain attacks.

Biometric authentication is another emerging method for IoT security, particularly for devices that involve human interaction. Smart home devices, wearables, and industrial control systems can use biometric identifiers such as fingerprints, facial recognition, or voice patterns to authenticate users before granting access. Biometric authentication offers a more seamless and user-friendly experience compared to passwords or PINs, but it also introduces privacy concerns and potential security risks. Biometric data, if not stored and transmitted securely, can be stolen and misused for identity fraud. To mitigate these risks, biometric authentication should be combined with strong encryption and stored locally on devices rather than in centralized databases that could become high-value targets for attackers.

Zero Trust authentication models are increasingly being adopted in IoT security. Unlike traditional authentication methods that rely on perimeter-based defenses, Zero Trust assumes that no device or user should be trusted by default, even if they are inside a protected network. Every access request is authenticated and continuously monitored based on contextual factors such as device behavior, location, and network conditions. This approach enhances security by reducing reliance on static credentials and requiring continuous verification of device identities. Implementing Zero Trust authentication in IoT requires advanced identity management systems, AI-driven anomaly detection, and encrypted communication channels to prevent unauthorized access attempts.

Blockchain-based authentication is another innovative approach to securing IoT devices. Blockchain enables decentralized identity management, allowing devices to register and authenticate themselves without relying on a central authority. Each device is assigned a unique blockchain identity that is immutable and verifiable across a distributed ledger. Smart contracts can enforce authentication policies, ensuring that only authorized devices can interact with the network. This method enhances security and resilience against identity spoofing and tampering. However, blockchain authentication requires additional computational resources and network bandwidth, making it less suitable for constrained IoT environments. Hybrid models that combine blockchain with lightweight authentication mechanisms are being explored to balance security and efficiency.

One of the biggest challenges in IoT authentication is managing identity credentials securely throughout a device's lifecycle. Devices must be authenticated not only during initial deployment but also throughout their operational lifespan, including software updates, ownership transfers, and eventual decommissioning. Secure credential storage and management are critical to preventing credential leaks and unauthorized access. Many IoT devices use hardcoded credentials in firmware, making them vulnerable to extraction and misuse by attackers. Secure elements, encrypted storage, and hardware-based authentication modules can help mitigate these risks. Additionally, implementing identity federation and dynamic credential issuance can improve security by ensuring that device identities remain verifiable even if their network conditions change.

Another key consideration for IoT authentication is the balance between security and usability. Many IoT devices operate in environments where human intervention is minimal or nonexistent, requiring fully automated authentication mechanisms. Traditional password-based authentication is impractical in such scenarios, as devices cannot manually enter credentials. Machine-to-machine (M2M) authentication methods, such as challenge-response protocols and mutual authentication, play a crucial role in ensuring secure interactions between autonomous devices. These protocols use cryptographic exchanges to verify identities without relying on human input, reducing the risk of credential theft or phishing attacks.

As IoT ecosystems continue to expand, authentication mechanisms must evolve to address emerging threats and scalability challenges. Future authentication models will likely incorporate AI-driven behavioral analysis, decentralized identity frameworks, and quantum-resistant cryptographic techniques to enhance security. Organizations deploying IoT solutions must carefully evaluate authentication mechanisms based on their specific security requirements, device capabilities, and operational environments. Ensuring that authentication processes are both robust and efficient will be essential for maintaining trust and resilience in interconnected IoT ecosystems.

Zero Trust Security in IoT and Edge Environments

The rapid proliferation of Internet of Things (IoT) devices and the shift toward edge computing have introduced new security challenges that traditional perimeter-based security models struggle to address. The traditional approach to network security assumes that everything inside the corporate firewall is trustworthy, granting broad access to devices and users once they have entered the network. However, in modern distributed environments, where devices and users interact across multiple networks, cloud services, and edge computing nodes, this assumption no longer holds. Zero Trust security has emerged as a more effective approach to protecting IoT and edge environments, enforcing strict authentication and continuous monitoring to ensure that no entity is trusted by default.

Zero Trust security operates on the principle that every access request, whether from a device, application, or user, must be verified before granting access to network resources. In IoT and edge environments, where billions of devices generate and process data outside centralized data centers, this approach is essential for preventing unauthorized access and mitigating cyber threats. Unlike traditional security models that rely on perimeter defenses such as firewalls and VPNs, Zero Trust assumes that the network is always hostile and that threats can originate from both internal and external sources. This means that security must be enforced at every layer, with authentication, authorization, and monitoring applied continuously.

A fundamental aspect of Zero Trust in IoT and edge environments is strong identity verification. Devices, users, and applications must authenticate themselves using multiple factors before being granted access. Traditional username-password authentication is insufficient for IoT devices, which often operate autonomously and lack user interfaces. Instead, Zero Trust frameworks rely on more advanced authentication mechanisms such as public key infrastructure (PKI), digital certificates, hardware security modules, and biometric authentication. Mutual authentication ensures that both the requesting entity and the receiving system verify each other's identities before establishing communication, reducing the risk of identity spoofing and unauthorized access.

Micro-segmentation is another critical component of Zero Trust security in IoT and edge environments. In traditional network architectures, once an attacker gains access to the network, they can often move laterally across different systems and devices. Micro-segmentation limits the ability of attackers to move freely by dividing the network into smaller, isolated segments. Each IoT device, edge node, and application is assigned its own security policies and access controls, ensuring that even if one device is compromised, the impact is contained. Micro-segmentation is particularly useful in industrial IoT environments, where operational technology (OT) systems must be isolated from IT networks to prevent cyber-physical attacks.

Continuous monitoring and anomaly detection are essential for maintaining Zero Trust security in IoT and edge environments. Since these environments involve highly dynamic interactions between devices, users, and cloud services, security teams must have real-time visibility into network traffic, authentication events, and device behaviors. Artificial intelligence and machine learning are increasingly being used to detect unusual patterns that may indicate a security breach, such as unexpected device communication, unauthorized access attempts, or deviations from normal operating behavior. By continuously analyzing identity and access data, organizations can respond to threats in real time and prevent potential security incidents before they escalate.

Zero Trust security also enforces the principle of least privilege, ensuring that devices and users only have access to the specific resources they need to perform their functions. In IoT environments, where devices often perform specialized tasks, granting broad or unnecessary permissions increases the attack surface. Access controls must be dynamic, adjusting in real time based on contextual factors such as device location, risk level, and recent activity. Attribute-based access control (ABAC) and role-based access control (RBAC) frameworks help enforce least privilege policies, ensuring that access rights are tightly regulated and continuously updated based on operational requirements.

Edge computing further complicates Zero Trust security by decentralizing data processing and decision-making. In traditional cloud environments, identity verification and access control are often managed by centralized authentication servers. However, in edge environments, computing resources are distributed across multiple locations, requiring local authentication and policy enforcement. This decentralized nature makes Zero Trust even more critical, as edge nodes must independently verify device identities, enforce security policies, and detect anomalies without relying on a central authority. Edge AI and federated learning models can enhance Zero Trust security by enabling devices to collaborate on threat detection and response without sharing sensitive identity data with external networks.

IoT devices present unique challenges for Zero Trust security due to their constrained computing resources and lack of built-in security features. Many IoT devices operate on low-power processors with limited memory, making it difficult to implement traditional security protocols such as full-scale encryption and complex authentication processes. Zero Trust frameworks must account for these limitations by leveraging lightweight authentication mechanisms, such as elliptic curve cryptography (ECC) and token-based authentication. Secure boot and firmware integrity verification further enhance Zero Trust security by ensuring that IoT devices only run trusted software and are not compromised during deployment or updates.

The adoption of Zero Trust security in IoT and edge environments also requires a shift in organizational mindset and security architecture. Unlike traditional security approaches that rely on implicit trust, Zero Trust demands continuous verification of every entity interacting with network resources. This requires organizations to implement identity-centric security policies, automate access control decisions, and integrate real-time threat intelligence into their security frameworks. Organizations must also consider regulatory and compliance requirements, as Zero Trust can help enforce data protection laws such as the General Data Protection Regulation (GDPR) and industry-specific security standards.

Zero Trust security in IoT and edge environments is not a one-time implementation but an ongoing process that requires continuous adaptation to emerging threats and evolving technologies. As IoT ecosystems expand and edge computing becomes more widespread, Zero Trust principles will play a crucial role in safeguarding critical infrastructure, protecting sensitive data, and preventing cyberattacks. By enforcing strong authentication, micro-segmentation, continuous monitoring, and least privilege access, organizations can build resilient IoT and edge environments that remain secure even in the face of sophisticated cyber threats.

Role-Based Access Control (RBAC) for IoT Devices

Role-Based Access Control (RBAC) is a widely used security model that regulates access to resources based on predefined roles within an organization. Originally designed for traditional IT systems, RBAC has become an essential framework for managing access control in IoT environments. As IoT ecosystems expand and devices interact autonomously with cloud services, edge computing nodes, and enterprise networks, implementing a structured access control mechanism is crucial to prevent unauthorized actions, data breaches, and security threats. RBAC offers a scalable and flexible approach to managing access by assigning permissions based on roles rather than individual users or devices. This reduces administrative overhead, enhances security, and ensures that access rights are consistently applied across diverse IoT infrastructures.

In IoT environments, devices often operate in various capacities, from collecting sensor data to executing critical system commands. Unlike traditional user-based access control models, IoT systems involve a combination of human users, automated processes, and machine-to-machine interactions. Without a well-defined access control mechanism, an IoT network could become vulnerable to privilege escalation attacks, unauthorized modifications, or data exfiltration. RBAC helps mitigate these risks by defining access policies that restrict devices and users to only the necessary functions required for their roles. By categorizing devices into different role groups, security administrators can enforce strict policies without having to manage access rights for each device individually.

One of the primary advantages of RBAC in IoT security is its ability to provide a hierarchical access structure. IoT networks typically include different layers of devices with varying levels of permissions. For example, in a smart home environment, a security camera may have different access rights than a thermostat or a smart lock. The security camera requires access to video storage and streaming services but should not have the ability to control heating or unlock doors. Similarly, in industrial IoT (IIoT) environments, a sensor that monitors temperature should not have the ability to modify system settings. By assigning appropriate roles to each device, RBAC ensures that devices cannot perform unauthorized actions beyond their designated responsibilities.

RBAC implementation in IoT environments involves defining roles, assigning permissions, and associating devices or users with these roles. Roles are predefined categories that group devices, users, or applications based on their function or level of trust. Permissions define the actions that a role is allowed to perform, such as reading data, writing configurations, executing commands, or accessing cloud services. For instance, in a healthcare IoT system, medical devices such as heart rate monitors may be assigned a role that allows them to collect patient data but not modify medical records. Doctors, nurses, and administrative staff may have different roles with specific access privileges based on their responsibilities. This structured approach reduces the risk of unauthorized access while maintaining operational efficiency.

RBAC also enhances security by enforcing the principle of least privilege, ensuring that each device or user only has access to the resources necessary to perform their tasks. This reduces the potential attack surface, limiting the impact of compromised credentials or malicious insiders. If an IoT device is hacked or compromised, RBAC prevents it from accessing resources beyond its designated permissions. For example, if an attacker gains control over a smart light bulb, RBAC ensures that the compromised device cannot access security cameras, door locks, or other critical systems. This containment minimizes the damage caused by security breaches and prevents lateral movement within the IoT network.

Scalability is another critical advantage of RBAC in IoT environments. As IoT deployments grow, managing individual access permissions for thousands or even millions of devices becomes impractical. RBAC simplifies this process by allowing administrators to modify roles instead of adjusting permissions for each device separately. If a new type of IoT sensor is added to an industrial facility, it can be assigned an existing role with predefined permissions instead of manually configuring access rights for each new device. Similarly, when devices are retired or replaced, they can be removed from their assigned roles without disrupting overall security policies. This approach streamlines access management and reduces administrative complexity, making it easier to maintain security at scale.

RBAC can also integrate with identity and authentication frameworks to strengthen IoT security. Combining RBAC with authentication mechanisms such as public key infrastructure (PKI), digital certificates, or biometric authentication ensures that only authorized devices and users can assume specific roles. Additionally, RBAC can be extended with dynamic access control policies that adapt based on real-time conditions. For example, an IoT device might be granted temporary elevated privileges based on environmental conditions, operational needs, or security alerts. In an industrial setting, a maintenance robot might be given access to restricted areas only during scheduled maintenance periods. By integrating RBAC with contextual and risk-based authentication, IoT security can be further enhanced.

Despite its benefits, implementing RBAC in IoT environments presents several challenges. One of the main difficulties is defining role hierarchies that accurately reflect the complexity of IoT deployments. Unlike traditional IT environments where roles are clearly structured around job functions, IoT devices often have overlapping functionalities and varying levels of autonomy. Defining access policies that accommodate these differences while maintaining security requires careful planning and continuous adjustments. Additionally, IoT devices have limited computational resources, making it difficult to implement sophisticated RBAC policies directly on devices with low processing power and memory constraints. To address this, organizations often implement RBAC at the network or cloud level, where centralized access control policies can be enforced without burdening individual devices.

Another challenge is ensuring interoperability between different IoT platforms and vendors. Many IoT ecosystems consist of heterogeneous devices from multiple manufacturers, each with its own security protocols and access control mechanisms. Without standardized RBAC frameworks, organizations may struggle to enforce consistent access policies across different IoT systems. Adopting industry standards such as OAuth, OpenID Connect, and XACML can help improve interoperability and facilitate RBAC implementation across diverse IoT environments.

RBAC in IoT environments must also account for evolving security threats and regulatory requirements. Data privacy laws such as the General Data Protection Regulation (GDPR) and the California Consumer Privacy Act (CCPA) impose strict guidelines on access control and data protection. Organizations deploying IoT solutions must ensure that RBAC policies comply with these regulations by restricting access to sensitive information, logging access events, and enabling audit trails for security monitoring. Regularly reviewing and updating RBAC policies is necessary to keep up with emerging threats and changing operational needs.

The adoption of RBAC in IoT security will continue to grow as organizations seek scalable and efficient ways to manage access control across expanding IoT ecosystems. By structuring access permissions based on predefined roles, organizations can enforce security policies that protect devices, users, and data from unauthorized access. As IoT environments become more interconnected and complex, integrating RBAC with advanced identity management systems, artificial intelligence-driven security analytics, and adaptive access control mechanisms will further strengthen IoT security frameworks. Ensuring that RBAC is implemented effectively will be a crucial step in building secure and resilient IoT infrastructures that can withstand evolving cyber threats.

Attribute-Based Access Control (ABAC) in Edge Computing

Attribute-Based Access Control (ABAC) is an advanced access control model that determines access permissions based on attributes associated with users, devices, and resources rather than predefined roles or static access lists. In traditional IT environments, access control mechanisms such as Role-Based Access Control (RBAC) rely on fixed roles assigned to users or devices, granting permissions based on hierarchical role structures. However, as edge computing expands and IoT ecosystems grow more complex, the limitations of static access control models become evident. ABAC offers a more dynamic and flexible approach to security by considering contextual factors, environmental conditions, and real-time attributes when granting or denying access.

In edge computing environments, where data is processed closer to its source rather than in centralized cloud infrastructures, security challenges become more pronounced. Edge devices often operate in highly distributed and heterogeneous networks, making it difficult to apply traditional access control models effectively. Unlike centralized architectures where security policies can be enforced through a single identity provider, edge computing requires decentralized enforcement mechanisms that adapt to the dynamic nature of devices, users, and applications. ABAC provides a solution by allowing security policies to be defined based on multiple attributes, including device type, location, time of access, security posture, and user identity.

One of the primary benefits of ABAC in edge computing is its ability to provide fine-grained access control. Instead of relying on predefined roles, access decisions are made dynamically based on real-time attributes. For example, in an industrial IoT setting, a maintenance engineer may be granted temporary access to specific edge nodes based on their current job assignment, device security status, and physical location within the facility. Unlike RBAC, which assigns broad access rights to a predefined role, ABAC ensures that access is contextually relevant and limited to the specific conditions at the time of the request. This reduces the risk of unauthorized access and enhances security in edge environments where devices and users frequently change roles and locations.

The dynamic nature of ABAC makes it particularly well-suited for edge computing environments that rely on machine-to-machine (M2M) communication. Many edge devices operate autonomously, exchanging data and executing commands without human intervention. Traditional access control mechanisms that require predefined permissions for each device interaction become impractical in such scenarios. ABAC enables policy-based access control decisions that are automatically enforced based on the attributes of the requesting device, the target resource, and the environmental conditions. For instance, an edge AI system analyzing real-time traffic patterns may grant temporary access to a connected vehicle's onboard sensors if the system determines that an immediate security risk is present. Once the risk is mitigated, access can be revoked without requiring manual intervention.

Security policies in ABAC can incorporate a wide range of attributes to enforce access decisions. User attributes may include identity verification status, security clearance level, or assigned job function. Device attributes can include operating system version, security patch level, manufacturer trust status, and real-time performance metrics. Environmental attributes may involve network conditions, geographic location, time of day, or ongoing security alerts. By leveraging a combination of these attributes, ABAC allows organizations to enforce highly customized access control policies that align with specific security and operational requirements.

Another advantage of ABAC in edge computing is its ability to support Zero Trust security principles. Unlike perimeter-based security models that assume trust based on network location, Zero Trust enforces continuous authentication and authorization based on real-time conditions. ABAC enables organizations to implement adaptive access policies that dynamically adjust to changing security risks. For example, an IoT-enabled medical device operating in a hospital network may have unrestricted access to patient monitoring systems during normal operation. However, if the device is detected operating outside the hospital's secure network, ABAC policies can automatically restrict its access until additional authentication measures are performed. This approach minimizes the risk of credential theft, insider threats, and lateral movement attacks.

Despite its advantages, implementing ABAC in edge computing presents several challenges. One of the key difficulties is the computational overhead associated with evaluating multiple attributes for each access request. Edge devices often have limited processing power, memory, and energy resources, making it challenging to execute complex access control policies efficiently. To address this limitation, organizations must implement lightweight policy evaluation mechanisms that optimize attribute-based decision-making while minimizing resource consumption. Caching frequently used access control decisions and leveraging edge AI models for anomaly detection can help reduce the computational burden on edge devices.

Interoperability is another challenge when deploying ABAC in edge computing environments. Edge networks often consist of a diverse array of devices from multiple vendors, each with its own security architecture and identity management framework. Ensuring that ABAC policies can be consistently applied across different platforms and communication protocols requires standardization efforts. Open security standards such as eXtensible Access Control Markup Language (XACML) and the Next-Generation Access Control (NGAC) framework provide a foundation for implementing ABAC policies across heterogeneous IoT and edge environments. Organizations must also integrate ABAC with existing identity federation mechanisms to enable seamless authentication across distributed edge networks.

Scalability is a critical factor in the successful deployment of ABAC in large-scale edge computing environments. Unlike traditional IT systems that manage access for a limited number of users and applications, edge networks may involve thousands or even millions of connected devices. Each device generates a continuous stream of access requests that must be evaluated based on real-time attributes. To ensure scalability, ABAC implementations should leverage distributed policy decision engines that operate at the edge rather than relying on centralized cloud-based access control servers. By distributing access control enforcement closer to the devices and data sources, organizations can reduce latency, improve performance, and enhance security.

As edge computing continues to evolve, the role of ABAC in securing access to distributed resources will become increasingly important. Organizations must adopt a proactive approach to access control by integrating ABAC with other security technologies, including behavioral analytics, AI-driven threat detection, and blockchain-based identity management. By implementing adaptive access policies that respond to real-time security conditions, organizations can reduce the risk of unauthorized access, data breaches, and cyberattacks in edge environments. Ensuring that ABAC policies are continuously updated, tested, and refined will be essential for maintaining a secure and resilient edge computing infrastructure.

ABAC represents a significant advancement in access control for edge computing by enabling fine-grained, dynamic, and context-aware security policies. Its ability to adapt to real-time conditions, support Zero Trust security principles, and provide granular access control makes it a powerful tool for securing IoT and edge environments. As the adoption of edge computing grows across industries, organizations must prioritize the implementation of ABAC to protect sensitive data, mitigate emerging threats, and ensure compliance with regulatory requirements. By leveraging attribute-based policies, enterprises can enhance security while maintaining the flexibility and efficiency needed for modern edge computing architectures.

Identity Federation for IoT Ecosystems

Identity federation is a crucial concept in modern cybersecurity, enabling seamless authentication and access control across multiple domains, organizations, and platforms. In traditional IT environments, identity federation allows users to authenticate once and gain access to multiple services without needing separate credentials for each system. This approach simplifies identity management, reduces the risk of password fatigue, and enhances security by relying on centralized authentication providers. As IoT ecosystems continue to expand, identity federation is becoming increasingly important to ensure secure and scalable identity management across diverse networks, devices, and cloud services. Unlike conventional enterprise systems that primarily authenticate human users, IoT identity federation must address the complexities of authenticating billions of connected devices, applications, and autonomous systems.

In an IoT ecosystem, devices frequently interact with multiple cloud platforms, edge computing nodes, and enterprise networks. Without a federated identity model, each device would require separate authentication credentials for each service it interacts with, leading to a fragmented and inefficient security landscape. Identity federation enables IoT devices to authenticate once using a trusted identity provider and gain access to various services without needing to reauthenticate each time. This approach reduces the administrative burden of managing device credentials while improving security by centralizing identity verification. By leveraging standardized authentication protocols such as OAuth, OpenID Connect, and Security Assertion Markup Language (SAML), identity federation allows IoT ecosystems to enforce consistent identity policies across different domains.

One of the primary challenges in implementing identity federation for IoT ecosystems is the diversity of devices and communication protocols. Unlike traditional computing environments where users authenticate using web browsers or enterprise identity providers, IoT devices come in various forms, including industrial sensors, smart home devices, medical wearables, and autonomous vehicles. Each type of device has different computational capabilities, security requirements, and communication methods. Some IoT devices have robust processing power and can support cryptographic authentication protocols, while others operate in resource-constrained environments with minimal security features. Implementing a federated identity framework that accommodates this diversity requires flexible authentication mechanisms that can scale across different types of devices and networks.

Another key challenge is ensuring trust between identity providers and relying parties in a federated IoT ecosystem. In traditional identity federation models, organizations establish trust relationships with identity providers that authenticate users on their behalf. In IoT environments, trust must be extended to a broader range of entities, including third-party cloud services, edge computing platforms, and device manufacturers. Without a robust trust model, malicious or compromised identity providers could grant unauthorized access to sensitive systems, leading to security breaches. Implementing decentralized identity trust mechanisms, such as blockchain-based identity verification and distributed ledger technology (DLT), can enhance the security of federated IoT identities by ensuring that identity transactions are transparent, tamper-resistant, and verifiable.

Scalability is another critical consideration in federated identity management for IoT. Traditional identity federation frameworks were designed to handle human users in enterprise environments, where authentication requests are relatively predictable and manageable. In contrast, IoT ecosystems involve billions of devices generating continuous authentication and authorization requests as they interact with cloud services, edge nodes, and other devices. Ensuring that federated identity systems can scale to handle this massive volume of authentication requests requires optimized identity management architectures, including cloud-native identity providers, distributed authentication mechanisms, and AI-driven identity analytics.

Interoperability between different identity federation frameworks is a major challenge in IoT security. Many IoT platforms and device manufacturers implement proprietary authentication methods that do not integrate seamlessly with other systems. Without standardization, organizations deploying IoT solutions may face difficulties in enforcing consistent identity policies across their ecosystems. Efforts to develop open standards for federated IoT identity management, such as the Fast Identity Online (FIDO) Alliance and the Decentralized Identity Foundation (DIF), are helping to improve interoperability and ensure that IoT devices can authenticate securely across different platforms. Adopting identity federation standards that support device-to-device authentication, cloud service integration, and decentralized identity verification can enhance security while reducing complexity.

Privacy is another significant concern when implementing identity federation in IoT ecosystems. Many IoT devices collect and transmit sensitive data, including personal health information, location data, and industrial control system logs. Federated identity frameworks must ensure that authentication and authorization processes do not expose sensitive identity data to unauthorized entities. Implementing privacy-preserving authentication mechanisms, such as anonymous credentials, zero-knowledge proofs, and differential privacy techniques, can help mitigate these risks. By allowing devices to authenticate without revealing unnecessary identity information, organizations can enhance security while maintaining compliance with data protection regulations such as the General Data Protection Regulation (GDPR) and the California Consumer Privacy Act (CCPA).

The integration of identity federation with edge computing further complicates IoT security. In traditional federated identity models, authentication requests are often processed by centralized identity providers located in cloud data centers. However, edge computing environments distribute computing power closer to data sources, requiring localized authentication and authorization mechanisms. Implementing federated identity management at the edge requires secure identity synchronization, decentralized identity verification, and lightweight authentication protocols that minimize latency and bandwidth consumption. By enabling edge nodes to act as identity intermediaries, organizations can reduce reliance on centralized authentication servers while maintaining robust security controls.

The role of artificial intelligence and machine learning in federated identity management is becoming increasingly important for IoT security. AI-driven identity analytics can enhance authentication processes by detecting anomalous access patterns, identifying potential security threats, and automating identity verification decisions. Machine learning algorithms can analyze device behavior, network traffic, and contextual data to determine whether an authentication request is legitimate or potentially malicious. By incorporating AI-driven security intelligence into federated identity frameworks, organizations can improve threat detection, reduce false positives, and enhance overall security posture.

Ensuring that federated identities are securely managed throughout the lifecycle of IoT devices is another challenge. Unlike human users, who have relatively stable identity attributes, IoT devices frequently change ownership, undergo firmware updates, and experience decommissioning events. Managing identity transitions securely requires automated identity lifecycle management, including secure identity provisioning, credential rotation, and deactivation of retired devices. Organizations must implement identity governance policies that prevent unauthorized access to decommissioned devices and ensure that identity credentials are revoked when devices reach the end of their operational life.

As IoT ecosystems continue to expand and become more interconnected, identity federation will play a crucial role in enabling secure, scalable, and interoperable authentication frameworks. Organizations must adopt federated identity management solutions that accommodate the unique challenges of IoT security, including device diversity, trust establishment, scalability, interoperability, privacy protection, and edge computing integration. By leveraging advanced authentication protocols, decentralized identity technologies, and AI-driven security analytics, organizations can enhance the security and efficiency of their IoT deployments. Establishing standardized and scalable federated identity frameworks will be essential for ensuring the long-term security and resilience of IoT ecosystems.

Multi-Factor Authentication (MFA) for IoT and Edge Devices

Multi-Factor Authentication (MFA) has become a cornerstone of modern security frameworks, providing an additional layer of defense beyond traditional username-password authentication. As IoT and edge computing devices become more prevalent in critical infrastructure, industrial automation, healthcare, and smart home environments, securing these devices with strong authentication methods is essential to prevent unauthorized access and cyber threats. Unlike traditional IT systems, where users can enter passwords and use mobile authenticator apps, IoT and edge devices require innovative approaches to MFA that account for device autonomy, limited user interaction, and constrained processing capabilities. Implementing MFA in these environments presents both opportunities and challenges, requiring adaptive authentication models that balance security, usability, and scalability.

In its simplest form, MFA requires users or devices to authenticate using at least two independent verification factors before gaining access to a system or service. These factors are typically categorized as something the user knows, such as a password or PIN, something the user has, such as a hardware token or mobile device, and something the user is, such as a fingerprint or facial recognition. While these traditional MFA mechanisms work well for human users, they must be reimagined for IoT and edge environments, where devices communicate autonomously without direct human intervention. The challenge is to implement MFA in a way that allows devices to verify their identities securely while minimizing the burden on users and maintaining operational efficiency.

One of the most promising MFA approaches for IoT and edge devices is certificate-based authentication combined with hardware security modules. Digital certificates issued through Public Key Infrastructure (PKI) serve as something the device has, proving its identity to other network components. The certificate is securely stored in a Trusted Platform Module (TPM) or Hardware Security Module (HSM), ensuring that even if the device is physically compromised, its authentication credentials cannot be easily extracted or cloned. When an IoT device or edge node attempts to connect to a network, it presents its digital certificate for verification. To add an extra layer of security, the authentication process can include a challenge-response mechanism that requires the device to sign authentication requests using its private key, preventing unauthorized entities from impersonating legitimate devices.

Time-based authentication tokens are another viable MFA method for IoT and edge security. While traditional MFA systems rely on users entering one-time passcodes generated on their mobile devices, IoT implementations can use synchronized time-based tokens stored in secure memory. When an IoT device initiates authentication, it must provide a dynamically generated token that matches the expected cryptographic value calculated by the authentication server. Since these tokens are continuously changing, attackers cannot reuse stolen credentials, significantly reducing the risk of credential-based attacks. This approach is particularly useful in edge computing environments, where devices frequently authenticate to different services without relying on a persistent connection to a centralized authentication server.

Biometric authentication is an emerging MFA method for IoT devices that involve direct human interaction. Smart locks, medical devices, automotive systems, and industrial control panels increasingly incorporate biometric authentication as an added security layer. A fingerprint scanner, facial recognition module, or even voice authentication system can serve as a biometric factor, ensuring that only authorized individuals can interact with the device. While biometric authentication enhances security by eliminating the need for passwords, it also raises concerns regarding data privacy and biometric data storage. Secure biometric processing methods, such as template-based authentication that does not store raw biometric data, can help mitigate these risks while maintaining security integrity.

Context-aware authentication is an advanced MFA approach that enhances security for IoT and edge devices by analyzing real-time environmental and behavioral attributes before granting access. This method evaluates factors such as device location, network conditions, recent activity patterns, and user behavior to determine authentication legitimacy. If an IoT device suddenly attempts to authenticate from an unusual location or shows abnormal behavior, the system can prompt for additional verification before granting access. For example, if a smart industrial sensor is expected to communicate from a factory environment but suddenly transmits authentication requests from an unrecognized network, the system can require secondary authentication factors before allowing data exchange. AI-driven authentication models can continuously learn from device behaviors to improve authentication accuracy and detect anomalies in real-time.

One of the significant challenges in implementing MFA for IoT and edge devices is the balance between security and usability. Many IoT devices operate in resource-constrained environments with limited computing power, making it difficult to implement complex cryptographic operations or frequent authentication challenges. Edge devices that require real-time processing cannot afford high-latency authentication methods that introduce delays in critical operations. To address this, lightweight authentication protocols such as Fast Identity Online (FIDO), Elliptic Curve Cryptography (ECC), and zero-knowledge proofs are being explored to enable strong authentication with minimal computational overhead. Adaptive authentication strategies that apply different authentication requirements based on device risk levels can further optimize security without disrupting operational workflows.

The scalability of MFA in IoT ecosystems is another key concern. Unlike traditional IT environments, where authentication is typically limited to a fixed number of users, IoT deployments may involve millions of devices requiring authentication. Managing MFA for such a vast number of devices demands automated credential provisioning, centralized identity management, and secure onboarding processes. Cloud-based identity providers and federated authentication systems can help streamline MFA deployment by enabling devices to authenticate through trusted intermediaries rather than requiring individual device-to-server authentication. Blockchain-based decentralized identity models are also being explored as an alternative to traditional MFA, allowing devices to authenticate without relying on a central authority while ensuring cryptographic trust through distributed ledger technology.

Interoperability between different authentication standards and protocols remains a challenge in securing IoT and edge environments. Many IoT devices operate across heterogeneous networks that involve multiple vendors, platforms, and cloud services, each with its own authentication requirements. Ensuring that MFA implementations can seamlessly integrate across different ecosystems requires adherence to open authentication standards and cross-platform compatibility. Standardizing MFA frameworks for IoT through industry collaborations and regulatory initiatives can help reduce fragmentation and improve overall security.

As the number of connected devices continues to grow, implementing robust MFA mechanisms for IoT and edge environments will be critical in preventing unauthorized access, credential-based attacks, and identity fraud. Organizations deploying IoT solutions must evaluate the specific authentication needs of their devices and users, selecting MFA methods that balance security, efficiency, and ease of deployment. By leveraging certificate-based authentication, biometric verification, context-aware security, and lightweight cryptographic techniques, organizations can establish a multi-layered authentication framework that protects IoT and edge devices from evolving cyber threats. The integration of AI-driven authentication analytics, blockchain-based identity management, and federated authentication systems will further enhance the effectiveness of MFA in securing IoT ecosystems. Ensuring that MFA solutions are scalable, interoperable, and adaptable to real-world IoT constraints will be essential in building a secure and resilient connected infrastructure.

Device Identity and Lifecycle Management

Device identity and lifecycle management are critical components of securing IoT and edge computing environments. As billions of connected devices interact across networks, ensuring that each device has a unique and verifiable identity is essential for preventing unauthorized access, data breaches, and security threats. Unlike traditional IT systems, where user identities are managed through centralized directories and authentication frameworks, IoT and edge devices require a decentralized and automated approach to identity management. Each device must be securely provisioned, authenticated, and continuously monitored throughout its operational lifecycle to ensure its integrity and prevent malicious exploitation.

The lifecycle of an IoT device begins at manufacturing, where it is assigned an initial identity that serves as its foundation for authentication and trust. This identity may be embedded in the device through a unique cryptographic key, digital certificate, or hardware security module. Ensuring that device identities are securely provisioned during manufacturing is crucial to preventing supply chain attacks, where malicious actors attempt to inject counterfeit or compromised devices into legitimate networks. Secure provisioning techniques, such as Trusted Platform Modules (TPMs) and secure enclaves, can provide hardware-based protection for storing and managing device identities. Organizations deploying IoT solutions must establish trusted relationships with manufacturers to ensure that devices receive unique and tamper-resistant identities before they enter the market.

Once a device is deployed, it must be securely onboarded into an operational environment. Device onboarding involves registering the device with an identity management system, verifying its authenticity, and assigning it access permissions based on its role within the network. Traditional onboarding processes, which require manual configuration and authentication, are not scalable for large-scale IoT deployments. Automated onboarding techniques, such as zero-touch provisioning (ZTP) and self-attestation protocols, enable devices to authenticate and enroll themselves in a network without human intervention. These methods use cryptographic verification to ensure that only authorized devices can join a network, reducing the risk of unauthorized access and identity spoofing.

As IoT devices operate within networks, their identities must be continuously monitored and managed to ensure compliance with security policies. Device identity management systems must track device attributes such as firmware version, security posture, network behavior, and access history. Continuous authentication mechanisms can enforce identity verification at regular intervals, preventing unauthorized devices from maintaining persistent access. Anomalous behavior, such as unexpected communication patterns or unauthorized access attempts, can trigger automated security responses, including identity revocation, quarantine, or remediation. Artificial intelligence and machine learning can enhance identity monitoring by analyzing real-time device behavior and detecting potential security threats before they escalate.

One of the most challenging aspects of device identity management is handling device updates and modifications throughout its lifecycle. Devices frequently undergo firmware upgrades, configuration changes, and security patches that may impact their identity credentials and authentication processes. Identity management systems must ensure that device identities remain intact and verifiable even as their software and hardware components evolve. Secure firmware update mechanisms, such as digitally signed updates and over-the-air (OTA) patching, can help maintain device integrity and prevent identity tampering. Organizations must implement identity governance policies that require devices to authenticate themselves before applying updates, ensuring that only authorized changes are made to the device's identity attributes.

Device ownership changes present another challenge in identity lifecycle management. In many cases, IoT devices are transferred between users, organizations, or environments, requiring a secure transition of identity credentials. Unlike human identity management, where user credentials can be revoked and reassigned, device identities must be carefully transferred without exposing sensitive authentication keys or access permissions to unauthorized parties. Secure device handover protocols, including cryptographic re-enrollment and identity delegation mechanisms, allow organizations to reassign device identities while maintaining security controls. Ensuring that previous owners cannot retain access to the device after transfer is essential for preventing unauthorized data access and security breaches.

Decommissioning and retiring IoT devices also require careful identity management to prevent security risks. When a device reaches the end of its operational life, its identity credentials must be securely revoked to ensure that it cannot be used for unauthorized access or exploited by attackers. Many IoT deployments fail to properly decommission devices, leaving inactive identities exposed to potential attacks. Secure decommissioning processes involve wiping device credentials, revoking authentication certificates, and disabling access privileges in identity management systems. Organizations must implement automated decommissioning workflows that prevent orphaned device identities from lingering within networks.

Interoperability is a significant consideration in device identity management, as IoT ecosystems often involve devices from multiple manufacturers, communication protocols, and security frameworks. Ensuring that device identities can be seamlessly managed across heterogeneous environments requires adherence to open standards and interoperable identity management solutions. Protocols such as Device Provisioning Protocol (DPP), Extensible Authentication Protocol (EAP), and OAuth 2.0 provide standardized methods for managing device identities across different platforms. Identity federation models, where devices authenticate through a trusted third-party identity provider, can further enhance interoperability while reducing the complexity of managing identities across multiple domains.

Regulatory compliance also plays a critical role in device identity management. Organizations deploying IoT solutions must adhere to data protection and security regulations that mandate secure identity verification, access control, and authentication practices. Regulations such as the General Data Protection Regulation (GDPR), California Consumer Privacy Act (CCPA), and industry-specific security standards impose strict requirements on how device identities are managed. Compliance frameworks often require organizations to implement logging and auditing mechanisms that track device identity changes, authentication events, and access control decisions. Ensuring compliance with these regulations not only strengthens security but also reduces legal and financial risks associated with identity-related security breaches.

As IoT adoption continues to grow, the importance of device identity and lifecycle management will become even more pronounced. Organizations must develop comprehensive identity management strategies that account for secure provisioning, onboarding, authentication, monitoring, updates, ownership transfers, and decommissioning. By leveraging strong cryptographic identity frameworks, automated lifecycle management tools, and AI-driven security analytics, organizations can ensure that IoT devices maintain a verifiable and secure identity throughout their operational lifespan. Implementing a robust identity management framework is essential for protecting IoT ecosystems from identity-based threats, unauthorized access, and security vulnerabilities. Properly managing device identities not only enhances security but also ensures the long-term reliability and integrity of IoT deployments across various industries and applications.

Identity Governance and Administration (IGA) for IoT

Identity Governance and Administration (IGA) is a critical component of identity and access management (IAM) that focuses on defining, enforcing, and monitoring identity policies across an organization. Traditionally, IGA has been applied to human users, ensuring that employees, contractors, and third parties have the appropriate access to systems and data while maintaining compliance with security policies and regulatory requirements. However, as the Internet of Things (IoT) continues to expand, the need for IGA frameworks that accommodate the unique challenges of device identities has become increasingly urgent. IoT ecosystems involve billions of connected devices that must be securely authenticated, authorized, and managed throughout their lifecycles. Implementing effective IGA strategies for IoT is essential for ensuring security, compliance, and operational efficiency in highly distributed environments.

Unlike human identities, which are typically associated with a single individual and managed through centralized directories, IoT devices require a more dynamic and automated approach to identity governance. Each IoT device must have a unique and verifiable identity that can be tracked, monitored, and controlled. Managing these identities at scale requires robust policies that define how devices are provisioned, how they authenticate to networks and services, what permissions they have, and how their access is modified or revoked over time. Without proper governance, IoT deployments can become highly vulnerable to security breaches, unauthorized access, and identity-based attacks.

One of the primary challenges in IGA for IoT is the lifecycle management of device identities. Devices must be securely provisioned with unique identities during manufacturing, onboarded into an organization's network upon deployment, and continuously monitored to ensure compliance with security policies. Over time, devices may require software updates, ownership transfers, or access changes based on evolving business needs. Without proper governance, these lifecycle events can introduce security gaps, such as abandoned or misconfigured devices that retain access to sensitive resources. Automating lifecycle management through identity governance frameworks ensures that device identities remain secure and up to date throughout their operational life.

Access control policies are a crucial aspect of IGA for IoT, defining what actions devices can perform and what resources they can access. Unlike human users, who can be granted access based on job roles, devices often operate autonomously and require predefined rules that govern their interactions. Implementing role-based access control (RBAC) or attribute-based access control (ABAC) models can help enforce least privilege principles, ensuring that IoT devices only have the necessary permissions to perform their designated functions. For example, an industrial sensor collecting temperature data should not have administrative access to modify network configurations. By enforcing granular access control policies, organizations can reduce the risk of compromised devices being used for lateral movement attacks within a network.

Auditability and compliance are critical components of IGA, requiring organizations to maintain visibility into device identities and their interactions with network resources. Many industries, including healthcare, finance, and critical infrastructure, are subject to regulatory requirements that mandate strict identity governance practices. Regulations such as the General Data Protection Regulation (GDPR), the California Consumer Privacy Act (CCPA), and industry-specific security frameworks impose requirements for tracking and managing device identities, enforcing data protection policies, and maintaining audit logs of access events. Organizations must implement robust identity governance solutions that provide real-time monitoring, logging, and reporting capabilities to ensure compliance with these regulations.

The integration of artificial intelligence (AI) and machine learning in IGA for IoT is becoming increasingly important for automating identity governance processes and detecting anomalies. AI-driven identity analytics can help organizations identify suspicious access patterns, detect unauthorized devices attempting to join the network, and flag high-risk activities that deviate from normal behavior. Machine learning models can analyze large volumes of authentication and access data to predict potential security threats and recommend policy adjustments in real time. By leveraging AI, organizations can enhance their ability to detect identity-related threats and enforce governance policies dynamically based on evolving security risks.

Identity federation plays a key role in IGA for IoT, enabling secure authentication across multiple domains and service providers. Many IoT ecosystems involve devices interacting with cloud services, edge computing nodes, and enterprise networks, often across different organizations and geographic regions. Implementing federated identity management allows devices to authenticate through trusted identity providers, reducing the need for multiple credentials while maintaining security and interoperability. Standardized identity federation protocols such as OAuth, OpenID Connect, and Security Assertion Markup Language (SAML) can help organizations enforce consistent identity governance policies across distributed IoT environments.

Another major challenge in IGA for IoT is securing identity credentials and ensuring that they are not exposed to unauthorized entities. Many IoT devices have limited processing power and storage capabilities, making it difficult to implement traditional security mechanisms such as multi-factor authentication (MFA) or complex cryptographic key management. Organizations must adopt lightweight authentication methods, such as certificate-based authentication and hardware security modules (HSMs), to securely store and manage device credentials. Implementing secure provisioning processes, such as embedding unique device identities in hardware during manufacturing, can prevent unauthorized modifications and ensure that devices can be securely authenticated throughout their lifecycle.

The scalability of IGA solutions is crucial in IoT environments, where organizations may need to manage millions of connected devices.

Traditional identity governance solutions designed for human users are not equipped to handle the vast number of identity transactions generated by IoT devices. Cloud-based identity governance platforms and distributed ledger technologies, such as blockchain, offer scalable solutions for managing IoT identities at scale. Blockchain-based identity management can provide tamper-resistant identity verification, enabling devices to authenticate and exchange credentials securely without relying on a centralized identity authority. By leveraging distributed identity frameworks, organizations can improve the scalability and resilience of their IGA implementations.

Governance policies must also address the decommissioning and disposal of IoT devices, ensuring that outdated or retired devices do not pose security risks. When a device reaches the end of its life, its identity credentials must be securely revoked to prevent unauthorized reuse or exploitation by attackers. Many organizations fail to properly decommission IoT devices, leaving abandoned identities in their networks that could be exploited for malicious purposes. Implementing automated identity revocation policies and secure data-wiping procedures ensures that decommissioned devices do not retain access to critical systems or sensitive information.

As IoT deployments continue to grow in scale and complexity, identity governance and administration will play an increasingly vital role in securing connected ecosystems. Organizations must implement comprehensive IGA frameworks that automate device identity lifecycle management, enforce granular access control policies, ensure compliance with regulatory requirements, and integrate AI-driven security analytics. By adopting scalable and interoperable identity governance solutions, organizations can enhance security, improve operational efficiency, and mitigate the risks associated with identity-related threats in IoT environments. Ensuring that devices are properly authenticated, monitored, and governed throughout their lifecycle is essential for maintaining the integrity and security of IoT deployments across industries and applications.

Security Standards and Regulations for IoT Identity

As the Internet of Things (IoT) continues to expand across industries, the need for robust security standards and regulations for device identities becomes increasingly critical. IoT devices are now integrated into every facet of daily life, from smart homes and wearable technology to industrial control systems and healthcare devices. With this widespread adoption comes the growing risk of security vulnerabilities, data breaches, and malicious cyberattacks. One of the key elements in ensuring the security and trustworthiness of IoT devices is the management of device identities. Securing these identities is crucial for protecting the integrity of IoT ecosystems and maintaining user privacy. To address the unique challenges of IoT security, governments, regulatory bodies, and industry organizations have introduced various standards and regulations that aim to safeguard IoT devices and their identities.

The fundamental goal of security standards for IoT identity is to ensure that devices can be uniquely and securely identified within a network. Device identities must be protected from manipulation, theft, or misuse, as they serve as the cornerstone for authentication and access control within IoT ecosystems. Without effective identity management, devices can be easily impersonated or compromised, potentially granting unauthorized access to sensitive data or systems. Security standards for IoT identity management must encompass various factors, including secure device authentication, data encryption, secure storage of credentials, and continuous monitoring of device behavior to detect anomalous activity.

One of the most widely recognized security standards for IoT is the IoT Cybersecurity Improvement Act, introduced by governments and regulatory bodies in response to increasing concerns over the security of connected devices. This act mandates the implementation of security controls that address device identification, authentication, and secure communications. It requires that IoT devices be designed to support secure boot processes, device authentication, and the use of secure cryptographic keys for identity management. By ensuring that devices have a unique, verifiable identity that cannot be easily spoofed, these regulations reduce the risk of unauthorized access and improve overall network security.

In addition to government-driven initiatives, the International Organization for Standardization (ISO) has developed a series of standards aimed at securing IoT devices, including ISO/IEC 27001 and ISO/IEC 27002, which focus on information security management systems. These standards provide guidelines for the implementation of secure IoT identity management practices, including the establishment of access controls, encryption methods, and secure authentication processes. ISO/IEC 29147 and ISO/IEC 30111 also provide frameworks for vulnerability handling and response, ensuring that any flaws in device identity management can be quickly identified and remediated. These ISO standards help establish best practices for secure device identity management and ensure that manufacturers adhere to globally recognized security protocols.

Another important regulation is the General Data Protection Regulation (GDPR), which enforces strict guidelines on the handling of personal data within the European Union (EU). GDPR has far-reaching implications for IoT device identity management, as it requires organizations to protect user data from unauthorized access and ensure that device identities cannot be exploited for malicious purposes. GDPR emphasizes the importance of user consent, data minimization, and the ability to revoke access at any time. For IoT ecosystems, this means that devices must be able to securely authenticate users and grant access based on predefined access policies. Any device that processes personal data, such as wearable health trackers or smart home devices, must ensure that its identity management system is in compliance with GDPR's privacy and security requirements.

The California Consumer Privacy Act (CCPA) provides similar protections for personal data in the United States. While CCPA is not specifically focused on IoT, it still imposes strict requirements on how businesses manage user data, including the identity and authentication mechanisms used by IoT devices. Like GDPR, CCPA mandates that organizations implement robust data protection measures, including secure device identities, to prevent unauthorized access to sensitive personal information. As IoT devices increasingly collect and transmit personal data, compliance with CCPA and other data privacy laws is essential for maintaining trust and ensuring that devices are properly secured.

Industry-specific standards also play a crucial role in securing IoT identities. For example, the Health Insurance Portability and Accountability Act (HIPAA) in the United States mandates specific requirements for securing healthcare devices, which often form part of IoT networks in medical settings. IoT devices used for patient monitoring or storing medical records must adhere to HIPAA's stringent identity and access management policies to ensure the confidentiality, integrity, and availability of patient data. This includes implementing secure device authentication mechanisms and ensuring that devices can securely store and transmit identity-related data. Similarly, the Payment Card Industry Data Security Standard (PCI DSS) applies to any IoT device that processes payment card information, requiring secure identity management to prevent identity theft and fraud.

One of the most significant aspects of security standards for IoT identity is the need for standardized device authentication protocols. Currently, there is no single, universal standard for IoT device authentication, leading to fragmented approaches that can create security vulnerabilities. However, initiatives like the Fast Identity Online (FIDO) Alliance are working to develop standardized authentication methods that can be universally applied across IoT ecosystems. The FIDO Alliance promotes the use of public key cryptography, biometric authentication, and other secure methods for device authentication. These standards enable devices to authenticate securely with minimal user intervention, reducing the risk of identity spoofing or credential theft. The adoption of universal authentication standards is essential for streamlining IoT security and ensuring that devices can securely interact with each other, regardless of their manufacturer or platform.

Beyond the technical aspects of device identity management, security standards for IoT also address operational considerations such as device lifecycle management and secure decommissioning. The National Institute of Standards and Technology (NIST) has developed guidelines for the secure lifecycle management of IoT devices, including recommendations for securely provisioning devices, updating their software and firmware, and securely decommissioning devices when they are no longer in use. Properly managing device identities throughout their lifecycle ensures that outdated or compromised devices cannot be exploited by attackers to gain unauthorized access.

As IoT adoption continues to grow, the importance of implementing strong security standards and regulations for device identity management will only increase. IoT ecosystems are highly dynamic, with devices regularly interacting across various networks and platforms. Without clear and enforceable standards, device identities could be easily compromised, leading to potential data breaches, service disruptions, and privacy violations. Governments, regulatory bodies, and industry organizations must continue to collaborate to develop and enforce security standards that address the unique challenges posed by IoT identity management. By adhering to these standards, organizations can ensure that their IoT deployments are secure, compliant, and resilient to emerging threats in an increasingly interconnected world.

Biometrics and Behavioral Authentication in IoT

Biometric and behavioral authentication methods have gained significant traction in modern security frameworks, offering advanced mechanisms for verifying user and device identities. In the context of the Internet of Things (IoT), where traditional authentication methods such as passwords and PINs are often impractical, biometrics and behavioral authentication provide an innovative and user-friendly solution for securing IoT ecosystems. As IoT devices continue to proliferate across industries, from healthcare and smart homes to industrial automation and financial services, ensuring that only authorized users and devices can access critical systems is paramount. By leveraging unique biological traits and behavioral patterns, biometric and behavioral authentication methods enhance security while reducing reliance on static credentials that can be easily compromised.

Biometric authentication relies on unique physical or biological characteristics to verify a user's identity. Unlike passwords or security tokens, which can be stolen, shared, or forgotten, biometric identifiers are inherently linked to an individual and cannot be easily replicated. Common biometric authentication methods include fingerprint recognition, facial recognition, iris scanning, voice recognition, and even palm vein scanning. These technologies are already widely used in consumer electronics, including smartphones, laptops, and access control systems, but their integration into IoT devices introduces new opportunities and challenges. IoT-enabled biometric authentication can be used in various applications, such as unlocking smart locks, securing medical devices, authenticating users in connected vehicles, and granting access to industrial control systems.

One of the key advantages of biometric authentication in IoT is its convenience and ease of use. Unlike passwords, which require users to remember and enter complex character sequences, biometric authentication allows seamless access with a simple scan of a fingerprint or face. This makes biometric authentication particularly useful in environments where quick and secure access is required, such as smart homes, hospitals, and corporate offices. IoT devices equipped with biometric sensors can authenticate users instantly, reducing friction while maintaining strong security. For example, a smart home system can use facial recognition to grant access to family members while denying entry to unauthorized individuals. Similarly, a connected medical device can use fingerprint authentication to ensure that only authorized healthcare professionals can operate it.

Despite its advantages, biometric authentication in IoT also presents significant security and privacy challenges. One of the primary concerns is the secure storage and transmission of biometric data. Unlike passwords, which can be reset if compromised, biometric data is immutable—if an attacker gains access to a user's fingerprint or facial scan, it cannot be changed. To mitigate this risk, biometric authentication systems must implement robust encryption and secure storage mechanisms. Many IoT devices use secure enclaves or Trusted Platform Modules (TPMs) to store biometric templates locally, ensuring that raw biometric data is not transmitted over the network. Additionally, privacy-preserving techniques such as homomorphic encryption and differential privacy can help protect biometric information from unauthorized access.

Another challenge in implementing biometric authentication for IoT is the need for reliable and accurate recognition. Biometric systems must be designed to account for variations in user appearance, environmental conditions, and sensor quality. Facial recognition, for instance, can be affected by changes in lighting, head position, or facial expressions. Similarly, fingerprint scanners may struggle with wet or dirty fingers, leading to authentication failures. To improve accuracy and reliability, modern biometric authentication systems use machine learning algorithms that continuously adapt to variations in user characteristics. These AI-driven models enhance the performance of biometric recognition while reducing the risk of false positives and false negatives.

Behavioral authentication offers another layer of security by analyzing user behavior and interaction patterns to verify identity. Unlike physical biometrics, which rely on biological traits, behavioral authentication examines dynamic characteristics such as typing speed, gait analysis, touchscreen gestures, mouse movements, and even heart rate variability. These behavioral traits are unique to each individual and can be used to establish a continuous authentication mechanism, ensuring that a user remains authenticated throughout a session. In IoT environments, behavioral authentication can enhance security by detecting anomalies and preventing unauthorized access based on deviations from normal behavior.

One of the key applications of behavioral authentication in IoT is continuous identity verification. Traditional authentication methods, such as passwords or one-time biometric scans, provide a single point of verification at login. However, once access is granted, there is no further verification to ensure that the authenticated user or device remains legitimate. Behavioral authentication enables continuous identity monitoring by analyzing real-time interactions and detecting changes that may indicate unauthorized access. For example, in a connected vehicle, behavioral authentication can analyze driving patterns to determine if the driver is the authorized user. If the system detects an unusual driving style or an abrupt change in behavior, it can trigger additional authentication checks or disable certain functions.

In industrial IoT environments, behavioral authentication can help prevent insider threats and unauthorized access to critical systems. Employees using connected machinery can be authenticated based on their usage patterns, movement patterns, or voice commands. If an unauthorized user attempts to operate equipment in an unusual manner, the system can automatically restrict access and alert security personnel. Similarly, in financial transactions conducted through IoT devices, behavioral authentication can analyze transaction patterns, typing behaviors, and biometric signals to detect fraudulent activity in real time.

Combining biometric and behavioral authentication can create a multi-layered security approach for IoT ecosystems. Multi-factor authentication (MFA) frameworks can integrate biometrics as a primary authentication factor while using behavioral analysis as a secondary verification method. For example, a smart home security system can use facial recognition for initial authentication and then analyze walking patterns to ensure that the individual moving through the home matches the authorized user. This approach enhances security by reducing the risk of biometric spoofing, where attackers attempt to use photos, masks, or voice recordings to bypass authentication systems.

Despite the benefits of biometric and behavioral authentication, widespread adoption in IoT is still limited by technical constraints, privacy concerns, and regulatory requirements. Many IoT devices have limited processing power and battery life, making it challenging to implement complex biometric and behavioral recognition algorithms. Additionally, data protection regulations such as the General Data Protection Regulation (GDPR) and the California Consumer Privacy Act (CCPA) impose strict guidelines on the collection, storage, and processing of biometric data. Organizations deploying biometric authentication in IoT must ensure compliance with these regulations by implementing data minimization practices, secure storage mechanisms, and user consent protocols.

As IoT security threats continue to evolve, biometric and behavioral authentication will play an increasingly vital role in protecting connected devices and systems. By leveraging unique physiological traits and behavioral patterns, these authentication methods provide a more secure and user-friendly alternative to traditional passwords and static credentials. However, successful implementation requires addressing security risks, ensuring privacy protection, and optimizing authentication mechanisms for resource-constrained IoT devices. The future of IoT security will likely involve the integration of AI-driven authentication models, privacy-enhancing technologies, and adaptive security frameworks that combine biometrics, behavioral analytics, and contextual intelligence to create a robust and resilient authentication ecosystem.

Public Key Infrastructure (PKI) for IoT Security

Public Key Infrastructure (PKI) is a foundational security framework that enables secure authentication, encryption, and data integrity in digital communications. In the context of the Internet of Things (IoT), PKI plays a critical role in securing device identities, ensuring trusted communication, and preventing unauthorized access. As IoT ecosystems continue to expand, with billions of devices connecting to networks and exchanging sensitive information, the need for a robust and scalable identity management solution becomes increasingly important. PKI provides a proven method for establishing trust in IoT environments by leveraging asymmetric cryptography, digital certificates, and certificate authorities (CAs) to authenticate devices and encrypt communications.

One of the key challenges in IoT security is ensuring that each device has a unique and verifiable identity. Unlike traditional IT systems, where users authenticate with usernames and passwords, IoT devices must rely on more secure methods to verify their identities without human intervention. PKI provides a structured framework for issuing, managing, and revoking digital certificates that serve as device identities. These certificates are issued by a trusted CA and contain cryptographic keys that enable devices to prove their authenticity when communicating with other devices, cloud services, or edge computing nodes. By using digital certificates, IoT devices can establish encrypted connections and prevent identity spoofing, man-in-the-middle attacks, and unauthorized access.

Asymmetric cryptography is at the core of PKI, utilizing a pair of cryptographic keys: a public key and a private key. The public key is shared openly and used to encrypt data or verify digital signatures, while the private key remains securely stored on the device and is used for decryption or signing operations. When an IoT device needs to authenticate itself, it presents its digital certificate, which includes its public key and is signed by a CA. The recipient verifies the authenticity of the certificate by checking the CA's digital signature, ensuring that the device is legitimate and trusted. This process eliminates the need for shared secrets, which are vulnerable to theft or leakage, making PKI a highly secure authentication method for IoT environments.

One of the primary benefits of PKI in IoT security is its ability to support secure device provisioning and onboarding. When a new IoT device is deployed, it must be securely registered with the network and assigned a unique identity. PKI enables automated certificate issuance, allowing devices to securely obtain and store digital certificates during the manufacturing process or initial network connection. This ensures that only authorized devices can join an IoT ecosystem, preventing rogue devices from gaining access. Secure device onboarding is particularly crucial in large-scale IoT deployments, where manually configuring each device would be impractical. PKI simplifies this process by enabling zero-touch provisioning, where devices automatically authenticate and enroll themselves into the network without requiring human intervention.

PKI also plays a critical role in ensuring data confidentiality and integrity in IoT communications. IoT devices frequently transmit sensitive information, such as personal health data, industrial control signals, and financial transactions, over networks that may be vulnerable to eavesdropping or interception. By using PKI-based encryption, devices can establish secure communication channels that protect data from unauthorized access. Transport Layer Security (TLS) and Secure/Multipurpose Internet Mail Extensions (S/MIME) are common PKI-based encryption protocols that help secure IoT data exchanges. Additionally, digital signatures generated using private keys ensure the integrity of transmitted data, allowing recipients to verify that messages have not been altered in transit.

Scalability is a significant consideration when implementing PKI in IoT security. Unlike traditional enterprise environments, where a relatively small number of users and devices require certificates, IoT networks involve millions or even billions of devices, each needing a unique digital identity. Managing such a vast number of certificates requires a highly efficient certificate lifecycle management system, capable of handling certificate issuance, renewal, revocation, and expiration. Automated certificate management platforms, integrated with PKI, help organizations scale their IoT deployments by streamlining certificate distribution and ensuring that devices always operate with valid and up-to-date credentials. Without proper certificate lifecycle management, expired or compromised certificates could lead to security vulnerabilities, such as unauthorized access or service disruptions.

Interoperability is another challenge in implementing PKI for IoT security. IoT ecosystems consist of devices from multiple manufacturers, each using different security protocols and communication standards. Ensuring that PKI-based authentication and encryption mechanisms work seamlessly across heterogeneous devices and networks requires adherence to open standards. The use of standard PKI protocols, such as X.509 digital certificates, Online Certificate Status Protocol (OCSP), and Certificate Revocation Lists (CRLs), enables interoperability between different IoT platforms and security frameworks. Industry organizations such as the Fast Identity Online (FIDO) Alliance, the Internet Engineering Task Force (IETF), and the Industrial Internet Consortium (IIC) are working to establish best practices for implementing PKI in IoT security to improve interoperability and trust across diverse ecosystems.

Despite its advantages, implementing PKI in IoT security presents several challenges. One of the primary concerns is the resource constraints of many IoT devices. Unlike traditional computing systems, which have ample processing power and storage capacity, many IoT devices operate on low-power microcontrollers with limited memory and computational resources. Performing complex cryptographic operations, such as key generation and certificate validation, can be resource-intensive, potentially impacting device performance and battery life. To address this challenge, lightweight cryptographic algorithms, such as Elliptic Curve Cryptography (ECC), are being adopted to provide strong security with reduced computational overhead. Additionally, hardware security modules (HSMs) and Trusted Platform Modules (TPMs) can be integrated into IoT devices to offload cryptographic processing and enhance security.

Another challenge in PKI implementation for IoT security is ensuring secure key storage and management. If a device's private key is compromised, its identity can be stolen and used for malicious purposes. Protecting private keys from unauthorized access requires secure storage solutions, such as secure enclaves or tamper-resistant hardware components. Secure boot mechanisms, which verify the integrity of device firmware before execution, can also prevent unauthorized modifications that could compromise PKI credentials. Organizations deploying IoT solutions must establish strict key management policies to ensure that cryptographic keys remain secure throughout a device's lifecycle, from manufacturing to decommissioning.

The role of PKI in IoT security will continue to grow as connected devices become more integral to everyday life and business operations. By providing a scalable and secure method for device authentication, encryption, and data integrity, PKI helps establish trust in IoT ecosystems and mitigates security threats. Organizations must carefully design their PKI implementations to account for the unique challenges of IoT environments, including scalability, resource constraints, interoperability, and key management. As IoT security evolves, advancements in PKI technologies, such as quantum-resistant cryptography and blockchain-based identity verification, may further enhance the security and reliability of IoT identity management frameworks. Ensuring that PKI remains a core component of IoT security strategies will be essential for building resilient and trustworthy connected systems across industries and applications.

Secure Identity Provisioning in Edge Computing

Identity provisioning in edge computing is a fundamental security process that ensures devices, applications, and users are authenticated and authorized before accessing network resources. As edge computing decentralizes data processing and moves it closer to the source, securing identity provisioning becomes more complex than in traditional centralized architectures. Edge environments often involve thousands or millions of distributed devices, each requiring a unique identity that can be securely managed throughout its lifecycle. Without a robust identity provisioning framework, edge deployments become vulnerable to unauthorized access, identity spoofing, and cyberattacks that can compromise the integrity of data and systems.

In edge computing, identity provisioning refers to the process of assigning, managing, and securing digital identities for edge devices, services, and applications. This includes generating cryptographic credentials, issuing digital certificates, and enforcing authentication policies that allow only authorized entities to interact with edge infrastructure. Unlike traditional identity management, which often relies on centralized identity providers, edge computing demands a distributed and scalable approach to identity provisioning. Devices at the edge frequently operate in dynamic environments where connectivity to cloud identity services may be intermittent or unavailable. This requires local identity verification mechanisms that can function autonomously while maintaining synchronization with central identity authorities.

One of the critical challenges of secure identity provisioning in edge computing is ensuring that devices receive their identities in a trusted manner. During the manufacturing or deployment phase, edge devices must be provisioned with unique credentials that cannot be tampered with or cloned. Hardware-based identity mechanisms, such as Trusted Platform Modules (TPMs) and secure elements, provide a strong foundation for secure provisioning by generating and storing cryptographic keys directly within the device. These hardware security modules protect device identities from extraction, ensuring that only legitimate devices can authenticate to the network. Secure boot processes further enhance identity provisioning by verifying the integrity of the device firmware and preventing unauthorized code from executing.

Automated identity provisioning is essential for scaling edge computing deployments. Traditional manual provisioning methods, such as configuring device credentials individually, are impractical in large-scale edge environments where thousands of devices may be added or replaced regularly. Zero-touch provisioning (ZTP) enables edge devices to securely enroll themselves into a network without manual intervention. When a new device is powered on, it automatically communicates with an identity provisioning service, verifies its authenticity, and retrieves its cryptographic credentials. This process ensures that devices are onboarded quickly while maintaining strong security controls. By eliminating the need for manual configuration, ZTP reduces the risk of misconfigurations that could expose edge systems to security vulnerabilities.

Public Key Infrastructure (PKI) plays a vital role in secure identity provisioning for edge computing. PKI provides a framework for issuing, managing, and revoking digital certificates that serve as unique identities for edge devices. Certificates are signed by a trusted certificate authority (CA) and enable secure authentication between devices, applications, and network services. When an edge device requests access to a resource, it presents its digital certificate, which is verified by the receiving system. This ensures that only authenticated and authorized devices can participate in edge networks. PKI-based identity provisioning also facilitates secure communication by encrypting data exchanged between devices, preventing eavesdropping and unauthorized interception.

Decentralized identity management models, such as blockchain-based identity provisioning, are emerging as a promising approach for securing identities in edge computing. Traditional identity management relies on centralized authorities to issue and verify credentials, which can create single points of failure. In contrast, blockchain-based identity systems distribute identity verification across a decentralized network, eliminating the need for a central authority. Each edge device is assigned a cryptographic identity recorded on a blockchain ledger, ensuring that identities cannot be altered or forged. Smart contracts automate identity provisioning by enforcing predefined security policies and granting access based on verifiable identity attributes. Decentralized identity provisioning enhances security, reduces reliance on central trust authorities, and enables cross-domain identity interoperability.

Identity federation is another critical aspect of secure identity provisioning in edge computing. Many edge environments involve multi-cloud and hybrid deployments, where devices and applications interact across different service providers and network domains. Federated identity management allows edge devices to authenticate with multiple systems using a single identity, reducing complexity and improving security. Standards such as OAuth, OpenID Connect, and Security Assertion Markup Language (SAML) enable seamless identity provisioning across diverse platforms. By federating identities, organizations can ensure that edge devices and applications can securely access cloud services, enterprise networks, and partner ecosystems without requiring redundant authentication processes.

One of the major security risks in identity provisioning for edge computing is ensuring that identity credentials remain protected throughout a device's lifecycle. Edge devices are often deployed in remote or physically exposed locations, making them susceptible to tampering, theft, or unauthorized modification. If an attacker gains access to a device's credentials, they could impersonate the device, access sensitive data, or inject malicious commands into the network. Secure key management solutions, including hardware security modules and encrypted credential storage, mitigate these risks by protecting private keys from unauthorized access. Additionally, periodic credential rotation ensures that compromised credentials cannot be used indefinitely.

Identity lifecycle management is an integral part of secure identity provisioning in edge computing. Once an edge device is provisioned with an identity, its credentials must be continuously monitored and updated as needed. Changes in ownership, software updates, and network reconfigurations may require identity modifications to maintain security compliance. When a device is decommissioned, its identity credentials must be securely revoked to prevent unauthorized reuse. Identity governance frameworks automate these processes by enforcing policies for credential expiration, renewal, and deactivation. Ensuring that edge devices maintain valid and up-to-date identities throughout their lifecycle reduces the risk of identity-based attacks and enhances overall security posture.

Artificial intelligence and machine learning are increasingly being integrated into secure identity provisioning systems to enhance security and automation. AI-driven identity analytics can detect anomalies in device behavior, flag suspicious provisioning requests, and prevent unauthorized access attempts. Machine learning models can analyze identity attributes, authentication patterns, and network behaviors to identify potential security threats in real-time. By incorporating AI-driven intelligence into identity provisioning workflows, organizations can strengthen their security defenses and adapt to emerging threats in edge computing environments.

Compliance with regulatory and industry standards is essential for secure identity provisioning in edge computing. Many industries, including healthcare, finance, and critical infrastructure, are subject to stringent security requirements that mandate secure identity management practices. Regulations such as the General Data Protection Regulation (GDPR), the National Institute of Standards and Technology (NIST) Cybersecurity Framework, and industry-specific security guidelines impose strict controls on how device identities are provisioned and managed. Organizations deploying edge computing solutions must ensure that their identity provisioning processes align with these regulations to protect user privacy, maintain data integrity, and prevent unauthorized access.

As edge computing continues to transform the way data is processed and managed, secure identity provisioning will remain a critical component of cybersecurity. The ability to securely assign, authenticate, and manage device identities at scale is essential for maintaining trust in distributed edge environments. Organizations must adopt robust identity provisioning frameworks that leverage PKI, zero-touch provisioning, decentralized identity models, and AI-driven security analytics to protect their edge computing infrastructure. By implementing these security measures, businesses can mitigate identity-related threats, enhance operational efficiency, and build resilient and trustworthy edge ecosystems.

Blockchain for Identity Management in IoT

The integration of blockchain technology into identity management for the Internet of Things (IoT) offers a revolutionary approach to securing device identities, enhancing trust, and decentralizing authentication processes. Traditional identity management systems rely on centralized authorities to issue and verify identities, creating single points of failure that are vulnerable to cyberattacks, data breaches, and operational inefficiencies. Blockchain provides a decentralized and tamper-resistant framework for managing identities across distributed IoT ecosystems, ensuring that devices, users, and applications can authenticate securely without relying on intermediaries. As IoT continues to expand across industries, blockchain-based identity management presents a promising solution to the challenges of scalability, security, and interoperability in connected environments.

One of the primary challenges in IoT identity management is establishing trust between billions of devices operating in decentralized networks. Traditional identity frameworks require IoT devices to register with central identity providers, which then validate authentication requests. This centralized approach introduces vulnerabilities, as a single compromised identity provider could jeopardize the security of an entire network. Blockchain eliminates this reliance on central authorities by distributing identity records across a decentralized ledger. Each IoT device is assigned a cryptographic identity recorded on the blockchain, ensuring that identities cannot be forged, manipulated, or revoked without authorization. By leveraging consensus mechanisms, blockchain ensures that identity records remain verifiable and secure without requiring a trusted third party.

Decentralized identity, also known as self-sovereign identity (SSI), is a core concept in blockchain-based identity management for IoT. With SSI, devices and users control their own digital identities without relying on external authorities for validation. Instead of registering identities with centralized servers, IoT devices generate their cryptographic keys and store identity attributes on a blockchain ledger. When authentication is required, devices can present verifiable credentials, which are cryptographically signed and validated by the blockchain network. This approach eliminates the risks associated with traditional identity management systems, where stolen credentials, data breaches, and insider threats can compromise security. Decentralized identity also enhances privacy by giving device owners full control over which identity attributes they share and with whom.

Another advantage of using blockchain for IoT identity management is its ability to provide tamper-proof audit trails. Traditional identity verification systems often lack transparency, making it difficult to detect fraudulent activities or unauthorized access attempts. Blockchain's immutable ledger records all identity transactions, providing a transparent and verifiable history of device authentications, identity updates, and access permissions. If a security incident occurs, organizations can trace identity-related activities back to their source, enabling forensic analysis and rapid response. This capability is particularly valuable in critical IoT applications such as industrial automation, healthcare, and supply chain management, where security and compliance are paramount.

Smart contracts enhance the automation and efficiency of blockchain-based identity management by enforcing predefined rules for authentication and access control. Smart contracts are self-executing programs stored on the blockchain that automatically verify identity credentials, grant or revoke access, and enforce security policies without human intervention. In an IoT ecosystem, smart contracts can facilitate dynamic identity verification processes, ensuring that devices only interact with authorized entities. For example, in a smart city infrastructure, a blockchain-powered identity system can use smart contracts to authenticate connected traffic sensors, streetlights, and surveillance cameras, allowing only verified devices to transmit and receive data. This reduces the risk of malicious devices infiltrating the network and ensures that only trusted components participate in critical operations.

Interoperability is a major challenge in IoT identity management, as connected devices often operate across multiple platforms, manufacturers, and communication protocols. Traditional identity solutions struggle to provide seamless authentication across diverse IoT ecosystems, leading to fragmented security policies and increased complexity. Blockchain enables universal identity interoperability by creating a standardized and decentralized identity framework that all devices can access. By using blockchain-based identity registries, IoT devices can authenticate across multiple networks and service providers without requiring separate identity credentials for each system. This is particularly beneficial in enterprise IoT deployments, where devices need to interact securely with cloud services, edge computing nodes, and industrial control systems managed by different entities.

Security and privacy remain significant concerns in IoT identity management, as compromised devices can be exploited for identity spoofing, data manipulation, and unauthorized access. Blockchain mitigates these risks by providing a decentralized and cryptographically secure identity framework that resists identity fraud and unauthorized modifications. Unlike traditional identity databases, which can be hacked or altered, blockchain's distributed ledger ensures that identity records remain immutable and verifiable. Additionally, blockchain-based identity solutions can incorporate zero-knowledge proofs (ZKPs), a cryptographic technique that allows devices to prove their identities without revealing sensitive information. This enhances privacy by enabling authentication without exposing device attributes or identity details.

Scalability is a critical factor in implementing blockchain-based identity management for IoT. While blockchain provides strong security guarantees, traditional blockchain networks face limitations in transaction throughput and processing speed. IoT ecosystems involve billions of devices generating continuous identity transactions, requiring a scalable blockchain architecture that can handle high transaction volumes efficiently. Emerging solutions such as sharding, off-chain identity verification, and layer-2 scaling protocols aim to address these challenges by improving the performance of blockchain identity systems. By optimizing transaction processing and reducing latency, these innovations enable blockchain-based identity management to scale effectively for large-scale IoT deployments.

Regulatory compliance is another important consideration for blockchain-based IoT identity management. Many industries, including healthcare, finance, and telecommunications, are subject to strict data protection regulations that govern identity security and privacy. Blockchain provides a transparent and auditable framework for identity compliance, ensuring that organizations can meet regulatory requirements while maintaining data integrity. By leveraging blockchain-based identity verification, organizations can enhance compliance with frameworks such as the General Data Protection Regulation (GDPR), the California Consumer Privacy Act

(CCPA), and industry-specific security standards. Blockchain's decentralized architecture also aligns with privacy-by-design principles, enabling IoT systems to enforce data protection policies while minimizing reliance on centralized identity repositories.

The adoption of blockchain for IoT identity management continues to evolve, with ongoing research and development efforts aimed at enhancing security, scalability, and interoperability. Industry consortia and standardization bodies, such as the Decentralized Identity Foundation (DIF) and the World Wide Web Consortium (W3C), are working to establish best practices for blockchain-based identity management. The integration of artificial intelligence and machine learning with blockchain identity solutions is also being explored to enhance threat detection, automate identity verification, and adapt to emerging security challenges. As blockchain technology matures, its role in securing IoT identity management will become increasingly important, enabling organizations to build trusted, decentralized, and resilient identity ecosystems for connected devices.

By leveraging blockchain's decentralized architecture, cryptographic security, and transparency, organizations can overcome the limitations of traditional identity management systems and establish a more secure foundation for IoT authentication and access control. The future of identity management in IoT will likely involve the widespread adoption of blockchain-powered identity frameworks, enabling seamless, tamper-proof, and privacy-preserving authentication across diverse connected environments. As IoT ecosystems continue to expand, blockchain's role in securing device identities will be instrumental in building a more secure and trustworthy digital landscape.

Identity Threat Detection and Response in IoT Networks

The rapid expansion of the Internet of Things (IoT) has introduced new security challenges, particularly in the realm of identity management. With billions of connected devices transmitting and processing sensitive data, identity-based attacks have become a significant concern for organizations deploying IoT solutions. Traditional security measures, such as perimeter defenses and static access controls, are no longer sufficient to protect against evolving cyber threats. Identity threat detection and response (ITDR) mechanisms are essential for identifying unauthorized access attempts, detecting identity spoofing, and mitigating malicious activities before they cause widespread damage. By implementing advanced monitoring, anomaly detection, and automated response strategies, organizations can enhance the security of their IoT networks and protect device identities from exploitation.

One of the most common identity threats in IoT networks is credential theft and identity spoofing. Attackers often attempt to compromise IoT devices by stealing authentication credentials, such as passwords, cryptographic keys, or digital certificates. Once an attacker gains access to a device's identity, they can impersonate it, gain unauthorized access to networks, and execute malicious commands. Unlike traditional IT environments, where identity theft typically targets human users, IoT identity theft focuses on devices and machine-to-machine (M2M) communications. To detect and respond to credential-based threats, organizations must implement continuous identity monitoring, encryption for stored credentials, and multi-factor authentication (MFA) mechanisms that prevent unauthorized access even if credentials are compromised.

Another major identity-related threat in IoT networks is unauthorized device enrollment. Many IoT systems use automated onboarding processes to provision new devices, allowing them to authenticate and join the network without human intervention. If these provisioning processes are not secured, attackers can exploit vulnerabilities to introduce rogue devices that masquerade as legitimate ones. These unauthorized devices can intercept network traffic, inject malicious code, or disrupt critical operations. To prevent unauthorized device enrollments, organizations must enforce strict identity verification protocols during onboarding. Using Public Key Infrastructure (PKI), device attestation, and certificate-based authentication ensures that only trusted devices can obtain network access. Automated threat detection systems can also monitor device enrollment activities and flag suspicious behavior, such as multiple failed authentication attempts or enrollment requests from unverified sources.

Anomaly detection plays a crucial role in identity threat detection and response in IoT networks. Since IoT devices operate autonomously, deviations from normal behavior often indicate potential security threats. Anomaly detection systems use artificial intelligence (AI) and machine learning algorithms to analyze device behavior, network traffic patterns, and authentication events in real time. If an IoT device suddenly begins transmitting large amounts of data, communicating with unapproved endpoints, or accessing restricted resources, the system can trigger an alert and initiate a response. By leveraging behavioral analytics, organizations can detect identity threats early and prevent attackers from exploiting compromised devices to gain further access to the network.

Identity-based attacks in IoT networks also include replay attacks, where attackers intercept legitimate authentication messages and retransmit them to gain unauthorized access. Unlike traditional brute-force attacks that attempt to guess passwords, replay attacks exploit weaknesses in authentication protocols to bypass security mechanisms. To mitigate this threat, IoT networks must implement cryptographic protections, such as time-based authentication tokens, nonce values, and session expiration mechanisms. These techniques ensure that authentication messages cannot be reused or manipulated by attackers. In addition, identity threat detection systems can monitor authentication attempts for signs of replay attacks, such as repeated authentication requests from the same source within a short period.

Compromised IoT devices can be weaponized for large-scale identity-based attacks, such as botnet infections. Attackers use botnets to take control of multiple IoT devices and orchestrate coordinated cyberattacks, such as distributed denial-of-service (DDoS) attacks, credential stuffing, and ransomware distribution. The Mirai botnet, for example, exploited weak IoT credentials to infect thousands of devices and launch massive DDoS attacks. To prevent botnet infections, IoT networks must implement strict identity access controls, disable default credentials, and continuously monitor for signs of compromised identities. Threat intelligence feeds and intrusion detection systems (IDS) can help organizations identify known botnet signatures and block malicious traffic before it spreads within the network.

Incident response strategies are essential for mitigating identity threats in IoT networks. When an identity-related security incident is detected, organizations must have predefined response plans to contain the threat and minimize damage. Automated response mechanisms can immediately revoke compromised device credentials, quarantine affected devices, and block malicious network traffic. Security orchestration and automated response (SOAR) platforms enable organizations to coordinate identity threat mitigation efforts across multiple security systems. By integrating real-time threat intelligence, automated remediation workflows, and forensic analysis tools, SOAR platforms enhance an organization's ability to respond swiftly to identity-based attacks.

Regulatory compliance is another important factor in identity threat detection and response for IoT networks. Many industries are subject to data protection laws and security regulations that mandate identity management best practices. Regulations such as the General Data Protection Regulation (GDPR), the National Institute of Standards and Technology (NIST) Cybersecurity Framework, and the California Consumer Privacy Act (CCPA) require organizations to implement secure identity authentication, logging, and access control mechanisms. Compliance audits and security assessments help organizations evaluate their identity threat detection capabilities and ensure they meet regulatory requirements. By aligning identity security policies with regulatory standards, organizations can reduce legal risks and improve overall cybersecurity posture.

The role of artificial intelligence and machine learning in ITDR for IoT is becoming increasingly critical. AI-driven security analytics can identify subtle identity threats that traditional rule-based security systems might miss. Machine learning models analyze vast amounts of authentication data, user behavior, and device interactions to detect suspicious activities and predict potential security incidents. Adaptive authentication mechanisms powered by AI can dynamically adjust access control policies based on real-time risk assessments. For example, if an IoT device exhibits unusual behavior, the system can require additional authentication factors before granting access or temporarily restrict its network privileges. By leveraging AI, organizations can enhance the accuracy and efficiency of identity threat detection while reducing false positives and security blind spots.

Identity deception techniques, such as deepfake biometric attacks and synthetic identity fraud, present emerging challenges for IoT security. As attackers develop sophisticated methods for bypassing authentication systems, IoT networks must evolve their identity threat detection capabilities to counter these threats. Continuous identity verification using multi-modal authentication, blockchain-based identity validation, and decentralized identity models can help improve resistance to identity deception attacks. Implementing biometric liveness detection, behavioral authentication, and device fingerprinting further strengthens IoT identity security.

As IoT networks continue to grow in scale and complexity, the need for advanced identity threat detection and response capabilities will only increase. Organizations must adopt proactive security strategies that integrate continuous monitoring, AI-driven anomaly detection, cryptographic protections, and automated incident response mechanisms. By implementing a comprehensive ITDR framework, organizations can protect their IoT ecosystems from identity-based attacks, prevent unauthorized access, and ensure the integrity of connected devices and data. The future of IoT security will depend on the ability to detect, analyze, and respond to identity threats in real time, ensuring that IoT deployments remain secure, resilient, and trustworthy.

Managing Third-Party Identities in IoT Environments

The management of third-party identities in IoT environments is a critical aspect of maintaining security, privacy, and operational integrity. IoT ecosystems often involve interactions between multiple stakeholders, including device manufacturers, service providers, suppliers, maintenance personnel, and external vendors. These third-party entities require varying levels of access to IoT devices, networks, and data, making identity management complex and challenging. Unlike traditional IT environments, where access control is largely limited to internal employees, IoT environments must extend identity management beyond organizational boundaries while ensuring that unauthorized entities do not gain access to sensitive resources.

One of the primary challenges in managing third-party identities in IoT environments is establishing trust between external entities and IoT systems. Each third-party organization or individual must be authenticated before they can access IoT devices or services. Traditional identity management models, which rely on username-password authentication, are insufficient for securing third-party access in highly distributed IoT networks. Instead, strong authentication mechanisms such as certificate-based authentication, public key infrastructure (PKI), and federated identity management must be implemented to ensure that only legitimate third parties can interact with IoT assets.

Access control policies play a crucial role in managing third-party identities in IoT ecosystems. Organizations must define granular access policies that specify what actions third parties are allowed to perform, what data they can access, and under what conditions they can interact with IoT devices. Role-based access control (RBAC) and attribute-based access control (ABAC) models provide structured approaches to defining and enforcing these policies. RBAC assigns third-party users and devices to predefined roles with specific permissions, ensuring that access is limited to authorized functions. ABAC extends this concept by incorporating contextual attributes such as location, device type, time of access, and security posture to make dynamic access control decisions.

Third-party identities often require temporary or conditional access to IoT systems. For example, a maintenance contractor may need to access an industrial IoT device for a limited time to perform diagnostics and updates. Once the task is completed, access should be automatically revoked to prevent unauthorized use of credentials. Temporary access management solutions, such as just-in-time (JIT) access and time-restricted authentication tokens, ensure that third-party access is granted only when necessary and expires after a predefined period. This minimizes the risk of credential misuse and unauthorized persistence in IoT networks.

Federated identity management enables seamless authentication and authorization of third-party identities across multiple IoT platforms and organizations. Instead of requiring third parties to maintain separate credentials for each IoT system they interact with, federated identity models allow external users and devices to authenticate using a trusted identity provider. Standards such as OAuth, OpenID Connect, and SAML facilitate secure identity federation, enabling third-party authentication while maintaining control over access permissions. Federated identity frameworks streamline identity verification, reduce administrative overhead, and enhance security by minimizing credential proliferation.

The integration of third-party IoT identities with cloud services introduces additional security considerations. Many IoT deployments rely on cloud-based platforms for data processing, storage, and remote management. Third-party vendors often require access to these cloud services to monitor device performance, deploy updates, or provide technical support. Cloud identity and access management (IAM) solutions help organizations enforce security policies for third-party access, ensuring that external entities only access cloud-based IoT resources according to predefined security policies. Implementing multi-factor authentication (MFA), least-privilege access controls, and continuous monitoring further strengthens the security of third-party interactions with cloud-hosted IoT assets.

Device identity verification is another important aspect of managing third-party access in IoT environments. Many third-party service providers interact with IoT devices remotely, making it essential to verify the authenticity of both the user and the device they are using. Device identity validation mechanisms, such as digital certificates, secure boot, and blockchain-based identity management, help ensure that third-party access requests originate from trusted sources. By binding third-party identities to verified devices, organizations can prevent identity spoofing, man-in-the-middle attacks, and unauthorized access attempts.

One of the major security risks associated with third-party IoT identities is supply chain compromise. IoT devices often pass through multiple suppliers, manufacturers, and distributors before deployment, creating opportunities for attackers to inject malicious code or tamper with device identities. Secure supply chain identity management involves implementing end-to-end device identity tracking, ensuring that each device maintains a verifiable identity from manufacturing to deployment. Blockchain technology provides a promising approach to securing supply chain identities by creating an immutable record of device identity transactions, allowing organizations to verify the integrity and provenance of third-party IoT assets.

Continuous monitoring and auditing of third-party identities are essential for detecting and responding to security incidents in IoT environments. Organizations must implement real-time identity monitoring systems that track authentication events, access requests, and identity-related anomalies. AI-driven identity analytics can help detect suspicious behavior, such as unusual access patterns, repeated authentication failures, or unauthorized privilege escalations. Automated identity threat detection and response mechanisms enable organizations to take immediate action when third-party identities exhibit signs of compromise, such as revoking credentials, isolating affected devices, or blocking suspicious access attempts.

Regulatory compliance plays a significant role in third-party identity management for IoT. Many industries, including healthcare, finance, and critical infrastructure, are subject to strict data protection regulations that govern third-party access to sensitive information. Regulations such as the General Data Protection Regulation (GDPR), the California Consumer Privacy Act (CCPA), and the Health Insurance Portability and Accountability Act (HIPAA) impose stringent requirements on how organizations manage and secure third-party identities. Organizations must implement compliance-driven identity management frameworks that ensure third-party access aligns with regulatory requirements while maintaining strong security controls.

The growing adoption of artificial intelligence (AI) and machine learning in IoT security is transforming third-party identity management. AI-driven identity verification systems analyze behavioral data, risk factors, and historical access patterns to make dynamic access decisions. Adaptive authentication techniques powered by machine learning can adjust third-party access permissions in real time based on evolving risk conditions. For example, if an external vendor attempts to access an IoT device from an unusual geographic location, the system can prompt for additional authentication factors or temporarily block access until further verification is completed. By incorporating AI-driven security intelligence, organizations can enhance the accuracy and efficiency of third-party identity management.

As IoT ecosystems continue to evolve, managing third-party identities will remain a critical challenge for organizations. Ensuring secure and controlled access for external entities requires a combination of strong authentication mechanisms, dynamic access controls, federated identity management, and continuous monitoring. By implementing comprehensive third-party identity governance frameworks, organizations can minimize security risks, protect sensitive IoT assets, and maintain regulatory compliance. The ability to securely manage third-party identities in IoT environments will be essential for fostering trust, enabling secure collaborations, and ensuring the long-term resilience of connected systems.

Identity-Based Encryption for IoT Security

Identity-Based Encryption (IBE) is an advanced cryptographic approach that enables secure communications by linking encryption keys directly to identifiable attributes, such as an email address, device identifier, or domain name. Unlike traditional encryption models that rely on pre-shared public keys and centralized key management, IBE simplifies key distribution and enhances security in decentralized environments like the Internet of Things (IoT). With billions of connected devices transmitting sensitive data across networks, securing IoT communications requires efficient and scalable encryption methods that do not impose excessive computational burdens. Identity-based encryption offers a promising solution by allowing IoT devices to encrypt and decrypt messages using dynamically generated cryptographic keys derived from identity attributes, eliminating the need for complex key exchange protocols.

One of the primary challenges in securing IoT networks is managing cryptographic keys at scale. Traditional public key infrastructure (PKI) requires a hierarchical certificate authority (CA) to issue, store, and validate public-private key pairs for every device, introducing significant operational complexity. In large-scale IoT deployments, where millions of devices need secure communication, this model can become inefficient, requiring frequent certificate renewals and revocations. Identity-based encryption eliminates the dependency on

CAs by allowing devices to generate encryption keys on demand using a trusted private key generator (PKG). This decentralized key management approach significantly reduces the overhead associated with distributing and maintaining encryption credentials, making IBE an ideal solution for resource-constrained IoT devices.

The core principle of IBE relies on mathematical functions that derive cryptographic keys from unique identity attributes. When an IoT device wants to encrypt data for another device, it uses the recipient's identity as the encryption key. The recipient, in turn, obtains a corresponding private key from the PKG, which allows decryption of the message. This approach eliminates the need for explicit key exchanges between devices, enhancing security by reducing the risk of key interception during transmission. Since IBE keys are identity-based, they provide a natural way to enforce access control policies, ensuring that only authorized devices can decrypt specific data. This is particularly useful in IoT environments, where devices from different manufacturers and networks frequently interact and require seamless authentication.

One of the advantages of IBE in IoT security is its ability to support fine-grained access control. Unlike traditional encryption methods, where access control is enforced through separate authentication mechanisms, IBE embeds access control directly into the encryption process. By associating encryption keys with specific identity attributes, organizations can define policies that restrict access based on role, location, device type, or operational context. For example, in a smart city environment, an encrypted message containing sensor data from a traffic monitoring system could be made accessible only to authorized government agencies while remaining unreadable to unauthorized third parties. This level of control enhances data security while enabling seamless communication across distributed IoT infrastructures.

Another important aspect of IBE is its ability to enable secure multicast and broadcast encryption in IoT networks. Traditional encryption models require separate key exchanges for each recipient, making large-scale data distribution inefficient. IBE simplifies this process by allowing a single encrypted message to be sent to multiple recipients based on their identity attributes. This capability is particularly useful in IoT applications such as smart grids, where energy usage data must be securely transmitted to multiple stakeholders, or in industrial automation, where command signals must be securely delivered to a group of devices. By eliminating the need for complex key distribution, IBE reduces latency and enhances the scalability of secure IoT communications.

Despite its advantages, implementing identity-based encryption in IoT environments presents certain challenges. One of the primary concerns is the reliance on a trusted private key generator. Since the PKG is responsible for generating private keys for all devices, it represents a potential single point of failure. If the PKG is compromised, attackers could obtain private keys and decrypt sensitive IoT data. To mitigate this risk, distributed PKG architectures and threshold cryptography techniques can be used to decentralize key generation across multiple entities, reducing the likelihood of a single compromised authority endangering the entire system. Implementing key rotation policies and periodic key updates further enhances security by ensuring that encryption keys remain resistant to long-term attacks.

Resource constraints in IoT devices also pose a challenge for IBE implementation. Many IoT devices operate with limited processing power, memory, and energy, making it difficult to perform complex cryptographic operations efficiently. While IBE eliminates the need for key exchanges, its encryption and decryption algorithms can be computationally intensive compared to traditional symmetric encryption methods. Optimizing cryptographic algorithms for IoT hardware, leveraging hardware-accelerated encryption modules, and adopting lightweight cryptographic variants of IBE, such as pairing-based cryptography, can help overcome these performance limitations. Balancing security and efficiency is crucial to ensuring that IBE remains a viable solution for real-time IoT applications.

Interoperability between different IoT platforms and identity management frameworks is another critical consideration for IBE deployment. IoT ecosystems often consist of heterogeneous devices from multiple vendors, each with its own authentication protocols and security standards. Ensuring that identity-based encryption seamlessly integrates with existing identity and access management (IAM) solutions, such as federated identity frameworks and blockchain-based identity verification, enhances compatibility across diverse IoT infrastructures. Standardizing identity attributes used for encryption, establishing interoperability guidelines, and adopting open cryptographic standards help facilitate seamless integration between IBE and existing security frameworks.

The use of artificial intelligence and machine learning in IBE-enabled IoT security is an emerging area of research. AI-driven analytics can enhance identity-based encryption by dynamically adapting encryption policies based on real-time threat intelligence. For example, if an anomaly is detected in network traffic patterns, an AI-powered security system could automatically adjust encryption policies to restrict access to sensitive data, mitigating potential security risks. Machine learning models can also assist in detecting identity spoofing attempts, identifying fraudulent authentication requests, and improving anomaly detection for IoT devices using IBE. Integrating AI-driven security mechanisms with identity-based encryption enhances proactive threat detection and response, further strengthening IoT security.

Regulatory compliance is another factor influencing the adoption of identity-based encryption in IoT security. Data protection regulations, such as the General Data Protection Regulation (GDPR) and the California Consumer Privacy Act (CCPA), impose strict requirements on data encryption and access control. IBE enables organizations to enforce compliance by embedding access control policies within encrypted data, ensuring that only authorized entities can decrypt sensitive information. By implementing IBE in IoT networks, organizations can meet regulatory mandates while enhancing security and protecting user privacy.

As IoT ecosystems continue to expand, identity-based encryption offers a scalable and flexible approach to securing device communications and protecting sensitive data. By simplifying key management, enabling fine-grained access control, and supporting secure multicast encryption, IBE addresses many of the challenges associated with traditional encryption models. While challenges related to key generation, computational efficiency, and interoperability remain, ongoing advancements in cryptographic research, AI-driven security analytics, and decentralized key management techniques are paving the way for broader adoption of IBE in IoT security. Establishing robust identity-based encryption frameworks will be essential for building secure, resilient, and privacy-preserving IoT environments.

Cloud vs. On-Prem Identity Solutions for IoT

The rapid expansion of the Internet of Things (IoT) has created an urgent need for robust identity management solutions that can authenticate, authorize, and manage connected devices securely. Organizations deploying IoT ecosystems must decide between cloud-based and on-premises identity solutions to control access and protect device identities. Both approaches offer distinct advantages and challenges, depending on the scale, security requirements, and operational needs of an organization. Cloud identity solutions provide scalability, automation, and seamless integration with distributed IoT networks, while on-premises identity management offers greater control, data sovereignty, and security customization. Understanding the differences between these two models is essential for designing a secure and efficient IoT identity framework.

Cloud-based identity solutions leverage cloud computing infrastructure to manage and authenticate IoT devices, users, and applications. These solutions provide centralized identity management, allowing organizations to authenticate devices remotely, enforce access control policies, and monitor identity-related activities from a unified dashboard. Cloud identity platforms use identity-as-a-service (IDaaS) models, which offer identity provisioning, multi-factor authentication (MFA), and role-based access control (RBAC) without requiring on-premises infrastructure. By outsourcing identity management to a cloud provider, organizations can reduce the complexity of maintaining identity servers, certificates, and encryption keys. Cloud-based solutions also integrate seamlessly with IoT cloud platforms, enabling real-time authentication and automated identity lifecycle management across distributed environments.

One of the key advantages of cloud identity solutions for IoT is scalability. IoT deployments often involve thousands or even millions of connected devices, each requiring secure identity provisioning and continuous authentication. Cloud platforms can dynamically allocate resources to accommodate growing identity demands without requiring manual intervention. Unlike on-premises solutions, which may require costly hardware upgrades to scale, cloud identity management systems can expand elastically, ensuring that organizations can handle large volumes of identity transactions efficiently. This scalability makes cloud-based identity management particularly beneficial for enterprises with geographically dispersed IoT deployments, where devices operate across multiple locations and networks.

Cloud identity solutions also enhance flexibility by enabling identity federation and cross-domain authentication. Many IoT devices interact with multiple cloud services, edge computing platforms, and third-party applications, requiring seamless authentication across diverse environments. Federated identity management, supported by cloud providers, allows IoT devices to authenticate once and gain access to multiple resources without needing separate credentials for each system. Standards such as OAuth, OpenID Connect, and SAML facilitate secure identity federation, reducing the administrative burden associated with managing separate authentication mechanisms for different services. This flexibility ensures that IoT devices can operate securely across hybrid and multi-cloud environments.

Despite these advantages, cloud-based identity solutions introduce concerns related to data security, privacy, and compliance. Many organizations, particularly those operating in highly regulated industries such as healthcare, finance, and government, must comply with strict data sovereignty laws that mandate local storage and processing of sensitive information. Cloud identity providers may store device credentials and authentication logs in remote data centers, raising concerns about regulatory compliance and unauthorized access. Additionally, cloud-based identity solutions rely on network connectivity to authenticate devices, which can pose challenges in IoT environments where intermittent connectivity or network disruptions may prevent real-time authentication.

On-premises identity solutions, in contrast, provide organizations with full control over identity management infrastructure. These solutions involve deploying identity servers, authentication systems, and access control frameworks within an organization's private data center or edge network. On-premises identity management is preferred in environments where data sovereignty, security customization, and offline authentication capabilities are critical. Organizations that handle highly sensitive IoT data, such as military, industrial, and critical infrastructure applications, often choose on-premises identity solutions to mitigate the risks associated with cloud-based identity management. By keeping identity data within internal infrastructure, organizations can enforce stricter security policies and reduce exposure to external threats.

One of the key benefits of on-premises identity solutions is enhanced security and control. Organizations have direct oversight of identity provisioning, authentication mechanisms, and encryption key management, allowing them to implement customized security measures tailored to their specific IoT deployments. Unlike cloud identity solutions, which rely on third-party providers for security enforcement, on-premises identity management enables organizations to define granular access control policies, enforce custom encryption protocols, and integrate identity management with existing cybersecurity frameworks. This level of control is particularly important for IoT systems that require stringent security measures, such as industrial control systems, medical devices, and autonomous vehicles.

On-premises identity solutions also offer reliability and independence from external service providers. In cloud-based identity management, authentication requests must pass through remote servers, creating potential latency issues and dependency on internet connectivity. If a cloud identity provider experiences downtime, IoT devices may be unable to authenticate or access critical services, disrupting operations. On-premises identity management eliminates these concerns by allowing organizations to authenticate devices locally, even in network-isolated environments. This capability is essential for IoT applications that require real-time authentication and access control, such as emergency response systems, autonomous robotics, and mission-critical industrial automation.

However, on-premises identity management comes with challenges, particularly in terms of scalability and maintenance. Deploying and managing an on-premises identity infrastructure requires significant investment in hardware, software, and skilled personnel. Organizations must maintain identity servers, update authentication protocols, and ensure that identity databases remain secure and up to date. Scaling on-premises identity solutions to accommodate growing IoT deployments can be resource-intensive, requiring additional server capacity and administrative overhead. Compared to cloud-based solutions, which offer automated identity provisioning and centralized monitoring, on-premises identity management may require more manual intervention and maintenance.

The decision between cloud-based and on-premises identity solutions for IoT depends on several factors, including security requirements, compliance obligations, scalability needs, and operational constraints. Some organizations adopt a hybrid approach, combining cloud and on-premises identity management to balance flexibility and control. In a hybrid identity framework, sensitive IoT assets may use on-premises authentication for critical operations, while less-sensitive devices leverage cloud-based identity services for scalability and ease of management. Hybrid identity solutions enable organizations to optimize security while taking advantage of the benefits of cloud-based automation and scalability.

Artificial intelligence and machine learning are increasingly being integrated into both cloud and on-premises identity management solutions to enhance security and automation. AI-driven identity analytics can detect anomalies in authentication patterns, flag unauthorized access attempts, and dynamically adjust access control policies based on real-time risk assessments. Machine learning models can analyze device behavior, authentication requests, and network interactions to identify potential identity threats before they escalate. Whether deployed in the cloud or on-premises, AI-powered identity management enhances threat detection, reduces false positives, and improves overall security posture.

As IoT ecosystems continue to evolve, the choice between cloud-based and on-premises identity solutions will remain a critical consideration for organizations seeking to secure connected devices. Cloud identity solutions provide scalability, automation, and seamless integration with distributed IoT networks, making them ideal for large-scale deployments. On-premises identity management offers greater control, security customization, and offline authentication capabilities, making it well-suited for mission-critical applications. Understanding the strengths and limitations of each approach enables organizations to design identity frameworks that align with their security, compliance, and operational objectives. By adopting a strategic approach to identity management, organizations can enhance the security and resilience of their IoT deployments while ensuring seamless and secure device authentication.

Identity Security in Industrial IoT (IIoT)

The Industrial Internet of Things (IIoT) is transforming manufacturing, energy, logistics, and other critical sectors by integrating smart devices, sensors, and automated systems to optimize processes and improve efficiency. Unlike consumer IoT, which focuses on convenience and automation for individuals, IIoT deals with large-scale, mission-critical infrastructure where security is paramount. Identity security in IIoT is essential for ensuring that only authorized devices, users, and applications can access industrial networks, preventing unauthorized access, data manipulation, and cyber-physical attacks that could disrupt operations. Managing identities in IIoT environments requires a combination of strong authentication mechanisms, secure access control policies, and continuous monitoring to detect identity-based threats.

One of the primary challenges in IIoT identity security is securing device identities across highly distributed industrial environments. Unlike traditional IT networks, where endpoints are typically limited to computers and mobile devices, IIoT networks consist of thousands or even millions of sensors, controllers, and industrial machines that must authenticate themselves before interacting with other systems. These devices often have limited processing power and storage capacity, making it difficult to implement traditional identity management solutions. Identity security frameworks for IIoT must account for these constraints while ensuring that all devices are uniquely identifiable and verifiable.

Public Key Infrastructure (PKI) plays a crucial role in establishing trusted identities for IIoT devices. PKI enables secure authentication by assigning digital certificates to each device, ensuring that communication between machines is encrypted and protected from tampering. When an industrial sensor or control system attempts to connect to a network, it presents its certificate, which is verified by a certificate authority (CA). This process ensures that only authenticated devices can participate in IIoT operations. PKI-based identity security also supports encrypted data transmission, preventing man-in-the-middle attacks and unauthorized data interception. However, deploying PKI at scale in IIoT environments requires automated certificate management to handle issuance, renewal, and revocation efficiently.

Another critical aspect of IIoT identity security is role-based and attribute-based access control. Industrial environments require strict access policies to ensure that only authorized personnel and devices can modify control settings or access sensitive data. Role-Based Access Control (RBAC) assigns permissions based on predefined roles, ensuring that engineers, operators, and maintenance personnel only have access to the systems necessary for their job functions. Attribute-Based Access Control (ABAC) enhances this by incorporating real-time contextual attributes such as device location, security posture, and operational status to make dynamic access control decisions. By enforcing least privilege principles, organizations can reduce the risk of insider threats and unauthorized device access.

Identity federation is becoming increasingly important in IIoT environments as industrial systems integrate with cloud platforms, edge computing, and third-party services. Traditional identity management models, where each system maintains its own identity repository, create inefficiencies and security risks. Federated identity solutions allow IIoT devices and users to authenticate across multiple systems using a single trusted identity provider. This simplifies authentication while maintaining strong security policies. Standards such as OAuth, OpenID Connect, and Security Assertion Markup Language (SAML) enable seamless identity federation, ensuring that industrial assets can securely interact with cloud analytics platforms, remote monitoring tools, and enterprise IT systems.

Zero Trust security principles are essential for protecting IIoT identity security. In traditional industrial networks, devices and users inside the network perimeter are often assumed to be trusted. However, this approach leaves systems vulnerable to lateral movement attacks, where attackers exploit compromised identities to gain deeper access to critical infrastructure. Zero Trust requires continuous identity verification, enforcing authentication and authorization checks for every access request, regardless of network location. Implementing Zero Trust in IIoT involves using multi-factor authentication (MFA), micro-segmentation, and continuous identity monitoring to prevent unauthorized access and detect anomalies in real time.

Machine-to-machine (M2M) authentication is another important aspect of IIoT identity security. Many industrial systems rely on automated communication between sensors, controllers, and cloud applications to operate efficiently. Ensuring that these interactions are secure requires strong M2M authentication protocols that prevent identity spoofing and unauthorized data exchange. Mutual authentication, where both communicating devices verify each other's identities before establishing a connection, is critical for preventing unauthorized devices from injecting malicious commands into industrial control systems. Lightweight cryptographic authentication protocols designed for resource-constrained IIoT devices ensure that security does not impact operational efficiency.

Identity lifecycle management in IIoT environments is crucial for maintaining security over time. Industrial devices often have long operational lifespans, requiring identity credentials to be managed from initial provisioning to decommissioning. Secure onboarding processes ensure that only trusted devices are added to IIoT networks, using hardware-based authentication mechanisms such as Trusted Platform Modules (TPMs) and secure boot processes to verify device integrity. Throughout their lifecycle, IIoT devices must have their identity credentials periodically updated to prevent security weaknesses. When a device reaches the end of its operational life, its identity credentials must be revoked to prevent unauthorized reuse or exploitation by attackers.

The integration of artificial intelligence and machine learning into IIoT identity security enhances threat detection and response capabilities.

AI-driven identity analytics can analyze authentication patterns, device behavior, and access logs to detect anomalies that may indicate compromised identities. For example, if an industrial control system suddenly starts communicating with an unauthorized external endpoint, AI-based monitoring tools can flag this behavior as suspicious and trigger an automatic security response. By continuously learning from device interactions, AI-driven identity security systems improve the accuracy of threat detection while reducing false positives.

Regulatory compliance is a major factor influencing identity security in IIoT. Industrial organizations must adhere to stringent cybersecurity regulations and industry standards to protect critical infrastructure and prevent cyber-physical attacks. Regulations such as the NIST Cybersecurity Framework, the European Union's Network and Information Systems (NIS) Directive, and the International Electrotechnical Commission (IEC) 62443 establish identity security guidelines for industrial systems. Compliance requires organizations to implement strong authentication, access control, and identity monitoring mechanisms to protect industrial assets from unauthorized access. Regular audits, security assessments, and identity governance frameworks help ensure compliance while strengthening overall IIoT security.

The convergence of IT and operational technology (OT) in IIoT environments introduces new identity security challenges. Traditionally, IT networks and industrial control systems operated separately, with different security requirements and identity management models. As IIoT connects these environments, organizations must integrate identity security across IT and OT domains to prevent cross-domain attacks. Identity security frameworks that bridge IT and OT enable unified authentication and access control, ensuring that industrial systems remain secure while enabling interoperability with enterprise networks.

As IIoT adoption continues to grow, organizations must prioritize identity security as a fundamental aspect of their cybersecurity strategy. The complexity of industrial networks, combined with the increasing threat of cyberattacks targeting critical infrastructure, makes it essential to implement strong identity authentication, access control, and threat detection mechanisms. By leveraging PKI, federated identity management, Zero Trust security, and AI-driven monitoring, organizations can protect IIoT assets from identity-based threats while ensuring the resilience and reliability of industrial operations. Building a secure identity framework for IIoT is essential for maintaining trust in connected industrial systems and safeguarding critical infrastructure against emerging cyber risks.

Privacy-Preserving Identity Management for IoT

The growing adoption of the Internet of Things (IoT) has raised significant concerns about privacy and data protection, as billions of connected devices continuously collect, process, and transmit personal and sensitive information. Traditional identity management models often require centralized databases that store user credentials, authentication logs, and access control policies, creating potential security and privacy vulnerabilities. In an era where data breaches, identity theft, and surveillance concerns are increasing, privacy-preserving identity management has become essential for protecting user and device identities in IoT ecosystems. Implementing privacy-centric identity frameworks ensures that IoT networks maintain security while minimizing the exposure of sensitive identity-related data.

One of the main challenges in IoT identity management is balancing authentication and authorization with privacy protection. Many IoT devices operate autonomously, requiring authentication to access services and communicate with other devices. Traditional identity verification methods often involve sharing identifiable information, such as usernames, device IDs, or cryptographic certificates, which can expose users to tracking and profiling. Privacy-preserving identity management techniques aim to authenticate devices and users while ensuring that personally identifiable information (PII) is not disclosed unnecessarily. This reduces the risk of unauthorized data collection, profiling by third parties, and potential exploitation of identity data for malicious purposes.

Zero-knowledge proofs (ZKPs) are a powerful cryptographic technique that enables privacy-preserving authentication in IoT environments. A zero-knowledge proof allows one party to prove knowledge of specific information, such as an identity credential, without revealing the actual data. For example, an IoT device can prove that it is authorized to access a system without disclosing its unique identifier or authentication key. ZKPs enhance privacy by ensuring that authentication can occur without exposing sensitive identity attributes. This approach is particularly useful in IoT applications where anonymous authentication is required, such as smart city infrastructure, healthcare monitoring, and decentralized access control systems.

Decentralized identity management, also known as self-sovereign identity (SSI), is another key approach to privacy-preserving identity management in IoT. Unlike traditional identity models, where central authorities issue and control digital identities, decentralized identity systems allow users and devices to manage their own identities through blockchain or distributed ledger technology. Each device or user is assigned a verifiable digital identity that is stored securely on a decentralized network, ensuring that identity data is not controlled by a single entity. When authentication is required, a device can present cryptographic credentials that prove its identity without relying on a centralized identity provider. Decentralized identity management reduces the risk of mass data breaches, enhances user privacy, and provides greater control over identity attributes.

Attribute-based credentials (ABCs) further improve privacy in IoT identity management by allowing devices and users to authenticate based on specific attributes rather than full identity disclosure. Instead of sharing complete identity information, an IoT device can present a verifiable claim that it meets certain authentication criteria without exposing unnecessary details. For example, a connected vehicle requesting access to a toll gate does not need to disclose its full registration information; instead, it can provide a cryptographic proof that it belongs to a valid class of authorized vehicles. This selective disclosure approach ensures that only the necessary identity attributes are shared, protecting user privacy while maintaining security.

Federated identity management models also contribute to privacy-preserving identity solutions by enabling cross-platform authentication without requiring centralized data storage. Federated identity frameworks allow users and devices to authenticate across multiple services using a single set of credentials, reducing the need for repeated identity verification. Privacy-enhancing federated identity systems use techniques such as anonymous credential issuance and tokenized authentication to prevent identity tracking across services. By minimizing the amount of identity data shared during authentication, federated identity management protects users from being monitored across different IoT networks and services.

Differential privacy is another advanced technique that can be applied to identity management in IoT. Differential privacy involves adding mathematical noise to authentication and identity-related queries to ensure that individual identity data cannot be extracted from aggregated datasets. This technique is particularly useful in IoT environments where identity analytics are used to detect anomalous behavior, manage access control, or enforce security policies. By ensuring that identity-related insights cannot be linked back to specific devices or users, differential privacy enables organizations to enhance security while preserving individual anonymity.

Secure multi-party computation (SMPC) is an emerging cryptographic approach that enables multiple parties to collaboratively process identity-related data without revealing the underlying information. In IoT networks where multiple entities, such as cloud providers, edge computing nodes, and service providers, participate in identity authentication, SMPC ensures that no single party has access to the full identity data. Instead, identity verification is performed through distributed computation, reducing the risk of identity exposure. This approach enhances privacy while enabling secure authentication and authorization in complex IoT ecosystems.

One of the biggest privacy risks in IoT identity management is the exposure of biometric data. Many IoT applications, including smart homes, healthcare devices, and industrial security systems, use biometric authentication methods such as facial recognition, fingerprint scanning, and voice authentication. While biometrics enhance security, they also introduce privacy concerns because biometric data is immutable and, if compromised, cannot be changed like a password. Privacy-preserving biometric authentication methods, such as local biometric processing and encrypted biometric templates, help mitigate these risks. Instead of transmitting raw biometric data to a central server, IoT devices can perform biometric authentication locally and store encrypted templates that prevent unauthorized access.

Regulatory compliance plays a crucial role in shaping privacy-preserving identity management in IoT. Data protection laws such as the General Data Protection Regulation (GDPR) and the California Consumer Privacy Act (CCPA) impose strict requirements on how identity data is collected, stored, and processed. Organizations deploying IoT solutions must ensure that their identity management frameworks comply with these regulations by implementing data minimization practices, strong encryption, and user consent mechanisms. Privacy-by-design principles, which emphasize embedding privacy protections into identity management systems from the outset, are essential for achieving regulatory compliance while maintaining security.

Artificial intelligence and machine learning are increasingly being used to enhance privacy-preserving identity management in IoT. AI-driven authentication systems can analyze behavioral patterns, network activity, and contextual factors to verify identities without relying on static credentials. Machine learning models can detect anomalies in identity authentication processes, identifying potential privacy threats while minimizing unnecessary identity disclosures. AI-powered identity management solutions enable adaptive authentication, where access control decisions are based on real-time risk assessments rather than predefined identity attributes. This approach improves security while ensuring that identity verification is dynamic and context-aware.

The future of IoT identity management will require a combination of decentralized identity frameworks, privacy-enhancing cryptographic techniques, and AI-driven security intelligence. By adopting privacy-preserving identity management solutions, organizations can protect user and device identities from unauthorized tracking, data breaches, and identity fraud. As IoT ecosystems continue to evolve, ensuring that identity management aligns with privacy principles will be essential for maintaining trust, compliance, and security in connected environments. Implementing robust privacy-preserving identity management strategies will allow IoT networks to scale securely while respecting user autonomy and data protection rights.

Self-Sovereign Identity (SSI) in Edge and IoT Systems

Self-Sovereign Identity (SSI) is an emerging paradigm that shifts control over digital identities from centralized authorities to individuals and devices, enabling greater security, privacy, and autonomy. In the context of edge computing and the Internet of Things (IoT), SSI provides a decentralized and tamper-resistant approach to managing identities across distributed environments. Unlike traditional identity management models that rely on centralized databases and third-party verification, SSI allows IoT devices, edge nodes, and users to create, manage, and authenticate their own identities using cryptographic credentials. This approach enhances security, reduces reliance on identity providers, and enables seamless authentication across heterogeneous IoT ecosystems.

One of the key challenges in IoT and edge computing environments is ensuring secure identity management without introducing centralized points of failure. Traditional identity verification systems require IoT devices to register with identity providers that control authentication and access. This creates security risks, as a compromised identity provider can expose all connected devices to attacks. SSI eliminates this dependency by enabling devices to generate and manage their own decentralized identities using blockchain or distributed ledger technology. By leveraging decentralized identifiers (DIDs) and verifiable credentials, IoT devices can authenticate without relying on a centralized authority, reducing attack surfaces and improving resilience against cyber threats.

Decentralized identifiers are a core component of SSI and play a crucial role in securing identity in IoT and edge systems. A DID is a unique, cryptographically verifiable identity that is not tied to any central registry, allowing devices to establish trust relationships independently. Each IoT device or edge node can generate its own DID and use it to sign authentication requests, proving its identity without exposing sensitive credentials. DIDs can be stored on decentralized ledgers, ensuring that identity data remains immutable and tamper-proof. When a device interacts with another system, it can present its DID and associated verifiable credentials, which are validated through cryptographic proofs rather than relying on external identity providers.

Verifiable credentials further enhance SSI by enabling IoT devices and edge systems to exchange authenticated identity attributes without revealing unnecessary information. Instead of sharing full identity details, devices can present cryptographic proofs that attest to their capabilities, security posture, or access rights. For example, an industrial IoT sensor could prove that it is authorized to transmit data to a factory's edge computing node without disclosing its entire identity history. This selective disclosure approach enhances privacy while maintaining strong authentication and access control mechanisms. By using verifiable credentials, IoT devices can establish trust dynamically, enabling secure interactions between machines, applications, and users.

One of the major advantages of SSI in edge and IoT environments is its ability to support offline and intermittent authentication. Many IoT deployments operate in environments with limited or unreliable connectivity, where traditional cloud-based authentication mechanisms may not function effectively. SSI allows devices to authenticate and verify credentials locally without requiring continuous access to a remote identity provider. Edge computing nodes can act as decentralized verifiers, ensuring that authentication processes remain secure even when cloud connectivity is unavailable. This capability is particularly valuable in critical infrastructure, remote industrial sites, and autonomous vehicle networks, where devices must operate independently while maintaining secure identity verification.

Another key benefit of SSI is its alignment with the principles of Zero Trust security. In traditional network security models, entities inside the network perimeter are often granted implicit trust, increasing the risk of insider threats and lateral movement attacks. Zero Trust requires continuous verification of every entity, enforcing authentication and access control at every interaction. SSI enables this approach by allowing each IoT device and edge system to authenticate dynamically using verifiable credentials. By implementing decentralized identity verification, organizations can establish trust in a Zero Trust environment without relying on centralized authentication authorities that could become single points of failure.

Privacy is a critical concern in IoT identity management, as many connected devices collect and transmit sensitive user data. SSI enhances privacy by ensuring that devices and users retain full control over their identity information. Unlike centralized identity systems, where personal data is stored in large databases that can be breached, SSI enables identity attributes to be stored locally and only shared when necessary. IoT devices can use privacy-enhancing technologies such as zero-knowledge proofs to prove identity attributes without disclosing raw data. This approach minimizes the risk of identity tracking, unauthorized profiling, and data leaks, making SSI a powerful tool for preserving privacy in IoT ecosystems.

Interoperability is another significant advantage of SSI in IoT and edge systems. Traditional identity management solutions often create silos, where devices and applications from different vendors require separate authentication processes. SSI provides a standardized identity framework that can be used across multiple platforms and ecosystems, ensuring seamless authentication across heterogeneous IoT networks. By adopting open identity standards such as the W3C Decentralized Identifiers specification and Verifiable Credentials, organizations can establish a universal identity layer that works across different IoT environments, cloud services, and edge computing infrastructures. This reduces complexity, improves efficiency, and enables secure cross-domain identity interactions.

Implementing SSI in IoT and edge computing requires a robust trust infrastructure, including decentralized identity registries, cryptographic key management, and identity governance frameworks. Blockchain and distributed ledger technology provide a secure and transparent mechanism for managing decentralized identities, ensuring that identity records cannot be altered or forged. Identity governance policies define how devices and users can create, update, and revoke identities, ensuring that SSI systems remain secure and compliant with regulatory requirements. Organizations must also implement secure key management practices, including hardware security modules (HSMs) and secure enclaves, to protect private keys associated with decentralized identities.

Regulatory compliance is an important consideration for SSI adoption in IoT environments. Data protection laws such as the General Data Protection Regulation (GDPR) and the California Consumer Privacy Act (CCPA) impose strict requirements on identity data management. SSI aligns with these regulations by giving users and devices control over their identity information, enabling data minimization, and ensuring that personal data is only shared with explicit consent. Organizations deploying SSI in IoT systems must ensure that their decentralized identity frameworks comply with regulatory standards, incorporating privacy-by-design principles to protect sensitive identity data.

Artificial intelligence and machine learning are increasingly being integrated into SSI frameworks to enhance security and automation. AI-driven identity analytics can detect anomalous authentication patterns, identify compromised devices, and recommend security policy adjustments in real time. Machine learning models can improve decentralized identity verification by analyzing trust relationships, device behaviors, and authentication logs to detect potential security threats. By combining AI with SSI, organizations can create adaptive and intelligent identity management systems that dynamically respond to emerging security challenges in IoT and edge computing.

The adoption of SSI in IoT and edge environments represents a fundamental shift in how identities are managed, authenticated, and secured. By eliminating reliance on centralized authorities, enhancing privacy, and enabling decentralized authentication, SSI provides a scalable and resilient approach to identity management in connected ecosystems. As IoT deployments continue to expand, implementing SSI will be essential for ensuring trust, security, and privacy across diverse and dynamic IoT infrastructures. Organizations must invest in decentralized identity frameworks, cryptographic security mechanisms, and interoperable authentication standards to fully realize the benefits of SSI in IoT and edge computing.

Secure Credential Storage and Management for IoT

The security of IoT ecosystems depends on the ability to securely store and manage credentials, including authentication keys, digital certificates, and cryptographic secrets. IoT devices require authentication to access networks, communicate with cloud services, and interact with other connected devices. If these credentials are exposed or compromised, attackers can gain unauthorized access, manipulate device functions, and even take control of entire IoT networks. Secure credential storage and management are critical to preventing credential theft, ensuring data integrity, and maintaining trust within IoT environments. The challenge is to implement security measures that protect credentials without imposing excessive computational or storage overhead, particularly on resource-constrained IoT devices.

One of the most common threats to IoT credential security is poor credential storage practices. Many IoT devices store authentication credentials in plaintext within device firmware, making them highly vulnerable to extraction. Attackers can use reverse engineering techniques to analyze firmware and retrieve hardcoded credentials, allowing them to impersonate devices or gain unauthorized access to networks. Secure storage mechanisms, such as hardware-based security modules, encrypted credential vaults, and tamper-resistant memory, are essential to protecting sensitive authentication data from exposure. By encrypting credentials before storage, organizations can prevent attackers from accessing them, even if they gain physical or remote access to an IoT device.

Hardware Security Modules (HSMs) and Trusted Platform Modules (TPMs) provide robust security for credential storage in IoT devices. HSMs are specialized hardware components designed to generate, store, and manage cryptographic keys securely. They prevent private keys from being extracted, ensuring that credentials remain protected even in the event of a device compromise. TPMs are integrated into many IoT devices and offer similar security capabilities by securely storing cryptographic keys and providing hardware-based authentication. By leveraging HSMs and TPMs, organizations can enhance the security of credential storage, reducing the risk of key theft and unauthorized access.

Secure Enclaves and Trusted Execution Environments (TEEs) further strengthen IoT credential security by isolating sensitive operations from the main device processor. TEEs create a protected execution environment where credentials can be securely processed without being exposed to the rest of the system. This prevents malware, rogue applications, or attackers from intercepting authentication keys or manipulating credential storage. Secure enclaves are used in advanced IoT security architectures to ensure that even if a device is compromised at the software level, its credentials remain inaccessible. The use of TEEs in IoT credential management improves resistance to advanced attacks, including memory scraping and side-channel attacks.

Key management is a crucial aspect of IoT credential security, ensuring that cryptographic keys are securely generated, distributed, rotated, and revoked. Static keys that remain unchanged for long periods present significant security risks, as attackers who gain access to them can exploit IoT devices indefinitely. Automated key rotation mechanisms ensure that keys are periodically updated, minimizing the risk of long-term credential compromise. Key revocation policies must also be enforced to disable compromised or outdated credentials, preventing unauthorized devices from using them to access networks. A centralized key management system or decentralized blockchain-based key distribution model can help organizations enforce strong credential governance across IoT deployments.

Credential lifecycle management ensures that IoT credentials remain secure from the moment they are created until they are no longer needed. The lifecycle of a credential involves several key phases, including provisioning, usage, renewal, and decommissioning. During the provisioning phase, secure enrollment processes must ensure that only authorized devices receive credentials. Credentials should be issued using secure channels, preventing attackers from intercepting them during transmission. Once in use, credentials must be monitored for anomalies, such as unauthorized access attempts or unusual authentication patterns. If a credential becomes compromised, it must be revoked immediately, and the affected device should be re-enrolled with new authentication keys.

Secure boot and firmware integrity verification mechanisms play a vital role in protecting IoT credential storage from firmware attacks. Secure boot ensures that only trusted firmware is executed during device startup, preventing attackers from injecting malicious code that could extract or manipulate credentials. Firmware integrity verification continuously monitors the device's software state, detecting any unauthorized changes that could indicate credential theft attempts. By combining secure boot with runtime integrity monitoring, organizations can ensure that IoT credentials remain protected from firmware-based threats.

Credential storage in cloud-connected IoT environments presents additional challenges, as cloud authentication mechanisms must protect credentials from remote threats. Cloud-based credential vaults provide a secure way to store and manage IoT authentication keys without exposing them directly to devices. Cloud identity services use encryption and role-based access controls to restrict credential access, ensuring that only authorized devices and users can retrieve authentication keys. Secure cloud integration requires IoT devices to authenticate using secure transport protocols, such as Transport Layer Security (TLS), which encrypts credentials during transmission and prevents interception.

Blockchain technology offers an innovative approach to secure credential management in IoT ecosystems by decentralizing identity verification and key distribution. Instead of relying on centralized key management authorities, blockchain-based credential storage enables devices to authenticate using distributed cryptographic ledgers. Smart contracts can automate credential issuance, renewal, and revocation, ensuring that IoT devices maintain secure identities without requiring constant interaction with centralized servers. Blockchain enhances credential security by providing tamper-resistant identity records, reducing the risk of credential forgery and unauthorized key modifications.

Regulatory compliance plays an important role in secure credential storage for IoT, as many industries must adhere to strict security and privacy requirements. Regulations such as the General Data Protection Regulation (GDPR), the California Consumer Privacy Act (CCPA), and industry-specific security standards mandate strong credential protection measures. Organizations must implement data encryption, access control policies, and audit logging to ensure that IoT credentials are managed securely and in compliance with legal requirements. Failure to protect IoT credentials adequately can result in regulatory penalties, legal liabilities, and reputational damage.

Artificial intelligence and machine learning enhance IoT credential security by enabling real-time anomaly detection and automated threat response. AI-driven security analytics can identify suspicious authentication attempts, detect credential misuse, and trigger automated mitigation actions. Machine learning models analyze historical authentication patterns, flagging deviations that may indicate credential compromise. By integrating AI into credential management frameworks, organizations can improve threat intelligence, strengthen authentication security, and reduce the risk of credential-based attacks.

As IoT deployments continue to expand, the importance of secure credential storage and management will only increase. Organizations must adopt robust security measures, including hardware-based key protection, automated credential rotation, and decentralized authentication models, to mitigate credential-related risks. Secure credential management frameworks ensure that IoT devices can authenticate securely while maintaining operational efficiency and compliance with regulatory requirements. By implementing strong encryption, advanced access controls, and intelligent threat detection, organizations can build a resilient IoT security infrastructure that protects sensitive authentication data from emerging threats.

Identity Attacks and Mitigation Strategies in IoT

The increasing adoption of the Internet of Things (IoT) has introduced new security challenges, particularly in the realm of identity management. IoT networks rely on the authentication and authorization of connected devices, users, and applications to prevent unauthorized access and ensure secure interactions. However, identity-based attacks targeting IoT environments have become a major cybersecurity concern. Attackers exploit vulnerabilities in authentication mechanisms, credential storage, and device identity verification to impersonate legitimate entities, manipulate data, and gain unauthorized control over IoT devices. Understanding these identity threats and implementing effective mitigation strategies is essential for securing IoT ecosystems against identity-related cyberattacks.

One of the most common identity-based attacks in IoT is credential theft. Many IoT devices rely on weak authentication mechanisms, such as default usernames and passwords, which attackers can easily exploit. Credential stuffing attacks involve using previously stolen credentials to gain unauthorized access to multiple IoT devices, taking advantage of the fact that users often reuse passwords across different systems. To mitigate credential theft, organizations must enforce strong password policies, implement multi-factor authentication (MFA), and regularly rotate credentials to reduce the risk of compromise. Secure credential storage using encryption and hardware security modules (HSMs) further protects authentication data from being accessed by attackers.

Identity spoofing is another major threat to IoT security. In an identity spoofing attack, an attacker impersonates a legitimate IoT device, gaining unauthorized access to network resources or injecting malicious commands. This type of attack is particularly dangerous in industrial and critical infrastructure environments, where compromised device identities can disrupt operations and compromise safety. Public Key Infrastructure (PKI) provides a strong defense against identity spoofing by enabling digital certificate-based authentication. Each IoT device is issued a unique digital certificate signed by a trusted certificate authority (CA), ensuring that only authenticated devices can communicate within the network. Mutual authentication further enhances security by requiring both communicating entities to verify each other's identities before exchanging data.

Man-in-the-middle (MITM) attacks exploit vulnerabilities in IoT identity authentication by intercepting communications between devices and altering transmitted data. Attackers may use MITM techniques to hijack authentication tokens, steal session credentials, or inject malicious payloads into IoT communications. Enforcing Transport Layer Security (TLS) encryption for all IoT communications mitigates MITM attacks by encrypting authentication exchanges and preventing unauthorized interception. Secure key exchange mechanisms, such as Diffie-Hellman key agreement and elliptic curve cryptography (ECC), further strengthen authentication security by ensuring that cryptographic keys are securely negotiated between devices without exposure to attackers.

Replay attacks are a specific type of identity attack in which an attacker captures legitimate authentication messages and replays them to gain unauthorized access. In IoT networks, replay attacks can be used to bypass authentication mechanisms and impersonate legitimate devices. Secure authentication protocols, such as time-based one-time passwords (TOTP) and challenge-response authentication, help mitigate replay attacks by ensuring that authentication messages expire after a short period or require unique responses for each authentication attempt. Nonce-based authentication mechanisms introduce random values into authentication requests, preventing attackers from reusing captured authentication data.

Insider threats pose a significant risk to IoT identity security, as attackers with legitimate access to IoT systems may exploit their privileges to manipulate device identities, escalate access rights, or leak authentication credentials. Insider threats can be difficult to detect, as they often involve authorized users or compromised devices that appear legitimate. Implementing Role-Based Access Control (RBAC) and Attribute-Based Access Control (ABAC) ensures that IoT users and devices have only the minimum permissions necessary for their functions. Continuous monitoring of identity-related activities using AI-driven anomaly detection helps identify insider threats by flagging suspicious access patterns, unauthorized identity modifications, and abnormal authentication behaviors.

Botnet attacks targeting IoT identity security have become increasingly common, with attackers hijacking large numbers of compromised IoT devices to launch coordinated cyberattacks. The Mirai botnet, for example, exploited weak IoT credentials to infect thousands of devices and use them for large-scale distributed denial-of-service (DDoS) attacks. Preventing botnet infections requires enforcing strong device authentication, disabling default credentials, and implementing automated credential rotation to prevent unauthorized persistence. Network segmentation further reduces botnet risks by isolating IoT devices into separate network zones, preventing compromised devices from communicating with critical infrastructure systems.

Identity attacks in IoT also extend to third-party and supply chain vulnerabilities. Many IoT deployments involve third-party service providers, device manufacturers, and software vendors that require access to authentication systems. If a third-party identity provider or supply chain partner is compromised, attackers can exploit their credentials to gain access to IoT networks. Implementing federated identity management with strong identity verification mechanisms reduces the risk of third-party identity compromise. Blockchain-based decentralized identity management further enhances security by eliminating reliance on central identity providers, ensuring that device identities remain secure even if a single entity in the supply chain is breached.

Zero Trust security models provide a comprehensive defense against identity-based attacks in IoT environments by enforcing continuous identity verification, micro-segmentation, and least-privilege access control. Instead of assuming that devices within a network perimeter are trusted, Zero Trust requires authentication and authorization for every access request, regardless of network location. Combining Zero Trust with adaptive authentication mechanisms, such as behavioral biometrics and risk-based access control, further strengthens IoT identity security by dynamically adjusting authentication requirements based on real-time security risks.

Artificial intelligence and machine learning play an increasingly important role in mitigating identity attacks in IoT networks. AI-driven identity threat detection systems analyze authentication logs, access patterns, and network behaviors to identify anomalies indicative of identity compromise. Machine learning models can detect unusual authentication attempts, credential misuse, and identity spoofing attempts in real time, enabling automated threat response mechanisms. AI-enhanced identity management systems improve threat intelligence, reduce false positives, and enhance security automation, helping organizations respond more effectively to emerging identity threats in IoT environments.

Regulatory compliance is essential for mitigating identity attacks in IoT, as industry regulations and cybersecurity standards provide guidelines for enforcing strong authentication and identity security practices. Regulations such as the General Data Protection Regulation (GDPR), the National Institute of Standards and Technology (NIST) Cybersecurity Framework, and the IoT Cybersecurity Improvement Act mandate security controls for IoT identity management, including encryption, access control, and identity governance. Ensuring compliance with these regulations helps organizations mitigate legal risks, enhance security posture, and protect IoT identities from exploitation.

Identity security is a fundamental aspect of IoT cybersecurity, requiring a combination of strong authentication mechanisms, cryptographic protections, Zero Trust architectures, and AI-driven identity monitoring. As identity attacks continue to evolve, organizations must adopt proactive security strategies that protect IoT credentials, prevent unauthorized access, and detect identity threats in real time. By implementing best practices for secure identity management, organizations can safeguard IoT ecosystems from identity-based cyber threats and ensure the integrity of connected devices, applications, and networks.

The Role of AI and ML in Identity Security for IoT

The integration of artificial intelligence (AI) and machine learning (ML) into identity security for the Internet of Things (IoT) has become essential in addressing the growing challenges of authentication, identity verification, and access control. As IoT ecosystems expand, traditional identity management solutions struggle to keep pace with the scale, complexity, and dynamic nature of connected devices. AI and ML provide advanced security capabilities by enabling real-time identity analytics, detecting anomalies in authentication patterns, automating access control decisions, and enhancing threat detection.

These technologies transform IoT identity security by improving accuracy, efficiency, and adaptability, making identity management more resilient against evolving cyber threats.

One of the key areas where AI and ML enhance identity security in IoT is anomaly detection. Traditional rule-based security systems rely on predefined authentication policies, which often fail to detect sophisticated identity attacks. AI-driven identity analytics analyze vast amounts of authentication data, device behavior, and network activity to identify deviations from normal patterns. Machine learning models can detect unusual login attempts, unexpected device movements, or irregular access requests that may indicate compromised credentials or unauthorized access. By continuously learning from historical authentication data, AI-powered anomaly detection improves over time, reducing false positives while accurately flagging potential security threats.

AI and ML play a crucial role in adaptive authentication, a security approach that dynamically adjusts authentication requirements based on real-time risk assessments. Instead of relying solely on static passwords or multi-factor authentication (MFA), adaptive authentication analyzes contextual factors such as device location, authentication history, network environment, and behavioral biometrics. If an IoT device exhibits normal behavior, AI-driven authentication systems may allow seamless access with minimal friction. However, if anomalies are detected, such as login attempts from unfamiliar locations or rapid changes in device behavior, the system can require additional verification steps, such as biometric authentication or one-time passcodes. This intelligent and risk-aware authentication process enhances both security and user experience by applying stronger security measures only when necessary.

Behavioral biometrics is another AI-powered identity security technique that enhances IoT authentication. Unlike traditional biometrics, such as fingerprint or facial recognition, behavioral biometrics analyze user interactions, including typing speed, touchscreen gestures, voice patterns, and movement habits. AI-driven behavioral analytics can create unique behavioral profiles for users and devices, allowing continuous identity verification without requiring explicit authentication. If an IoT device or user suddenly deviates from normal behavior, AI-based authentication systems can detect the anomaly and take action, such as temporarily blocking access or requesting additional verification. Behavioral biometrics strengthen identity security by making authentication more context-aware and resistant to credential theft or identity spoofing.

AI and ML improve role-based and attribute-based access control (RBAC and ABAC) by dynamically adjusting access permissions based on real-time data. Traditional access control models rely on static roles and permissions, which may not adapt to changing security conditions. AI-driven identity management continuously analyzes user and device behavior, adjusting access rights in response to evolving security threats. If an IoT device or user exhibits suspicious activity, ML-based access control systems can automatically restrict privileges, revoke access, or initiate additional authentication challenges. This dynamic and automated approach to access control minimizes the risk of unauthorized access while ensuring that legitimate users and devices can operate efficiently.

Identity fraud detection in IoT networks benefits significantly from AI and ML. Attackers often attempt to impersonate legitimate devices or users by exploiting stolen credentials, forging authentication requests, or hijacking device identities. AI-powered fraud detection systems analyze identity-related transactions, authentication logs, and behavioral data to identify fraudulent patterns. Machine learning algorithms can detect signs of credential stuffing, identity spoofing, and synthetic identity fraud by recognizing subtle indicators of malicious behavior. By continuously refining fraud detection models based on real-world attack data, AI-driven identity security systems improve their ability to identify and prevent fraudulent identity activities in IoT environments.

AI and ML enhance identity governance and compliance in IoT by automating identity audits, enforcing regulatory policies, and monitoring identity-related activities. IoT deployments must comply with data protection regulations such as the General Data Protection Regulation (GDPR), the California Consumer Privacy Act (CCPA), and industry-specific security standards. AI-powered identity governance solutions analyze identity access patterns, detect policy violations, and generate automated compliance reports. By using ML algorithms to identify anomalies in identity permissions and authentication behaviors, organizations can proactively enforce security policies and reduce the risk of compliance violations. AI-driven automation streamlines identity governance, reducing the administrative burden associated with manual compliance checks.

The use of AI in IoT identity threat intelligence strengthens security by predicting emerging identity-based attacks and recommending proactive mitigation strategies. Machine learning models can analyze global identity threat intelligence data, identifying patterns associated with credential breaches, account takeovers, and identity fraud campaigns. AI-driven security platforms integrate threat intelligence feeds to detect indicators of compromise (IoC) related to identity attacks, allowing organizations to respond quickly to emerging threats. By leveraging predictive analytics, AI-powered identity security solutions can anticipate potential identity risks and implement preemptive security measures before attacks occur.

Blockchain and AI integration in identity security further enhances trust and decentralization in IoT authentication. Decentralized identity management using blockchain provides tamper-proof identity verification, ensuring that device identities remain secure and immutable. AI enhances blockchain-based identity security by analyzing transaction patterns, detecting fraudulent identity registrations, and ensuring compliance with decentralized authentication protocols. By combining AI-driven threat detection with blockchain's transparent and verifiable identity records, IoT networks can achieve higher levels of identity security and trustworthiness.

AI-driven automation improves the efficiency of identity lifecycle management in IoT, reducing the risk of credential mismanagement and unauthorized access. Traditional identity lifecycle processes, such as credential provisioning, revocation, and renewal, often require manual intervention. AI-powered identity management automates these processes by detecting inactive or compromised identities, recommending credential updates, and dynamically adjusting authentication policies. Automated identity lifecycle management ensures that IoT devices maintain secure identities throughout their operational lifespan, preventing unauthorized access due to outdated or misconfigured credentials.

Federated identity management in IoT benefits from AI and ML by enabling seamless cross-domain authentication and identity verification. IoT ecosystems often involve multiple cloud providers, edge computing platforms, and third-party service integrations, requiring a unified identity framework. AI enhances federated identity authentication by analyzing authentication requests, detecting anomalies in cross-platform identity interactions, and ensuring that identity federation policies are enforced securely. By integrating AI into federated identity management, organizations can improve interoperability, reduce identity fragmentation, and strengthen security across diverse IoT environments.

As IoT adoption continues to grow, AI and ML will play an increasingly vital role in securing identity authentication, access control, and identity governance. These technologies provide real-time anomaly detection, adaptive authentication, and automated identity threat intelligence, making identity security more robust and scalable. By leveraging AI-driven security analytics, organizations can proactively detect identity attacks, enhance authentication accuracy, and implement intelligent identity management strategies that adapt to evolving security risks. The integration of AI and ML into IoT identity security will continue to shape the future of connected ecosystems, ensuring that identity verification remains strong, resilient, and efficient in an increasingly complex digital landscape.

Identity Security for Consumer IoT Devices

Consumer Internet of Things (IoT) devices have become an integral part of daily life, ranging from smart home assistants, security cameras, and wearable fitness trackers to connected appliances, smart TVs, and automated lighting systems. These devices enhance convenience, automate tasks, and improve efficiency, but they also introduce significant security risks. Unlike traditional computing systems, consumer IoT devices often lack robust identity management mechanisms, making them vulnerable to unauthorized access, identity spoofing, and data breaches. Ensuring strong identity security for consumer IoT devices is essential to protect user privacy, prevent cyber threats, and maintain the integrity of connected ecosystems.

One of the primary challenges in securing consumer IoT identities is weak authentication mechanisms. Many consumer IoT devices rely on default usernames and passwords, which are often never changed by users, making them an easy target for cybercriminals. Attackers frequently exploit weak credentials through brute-force attacks, credential stuffing, and dictionary attacks to gain unauthorized access to devices. To mitigate this risk, manufacturers and users must enforce strong authentication practices. This includes requiring complex, unique passwords for each device, implementing passwordless authentication mechanisms such as biometrics or cryptographic keys, and using multi-factor authentication (MFA) to add an extra layer of security.

Device identity spoofing is another critical threat in consumer IoT security. Attackers can impersonate a legitimate IoT device to trick users into granting access or intercepting sensitive information. For example, a malicious actor could create a rogue smart home device that mimics the identity of an existing device to infiltrate a network. Implementing Public Key Infrastructure (PKI) for consumer IoT devices can prevent identity spoofing by using digital certificates to authenticate devices. Secure device onboarding, where each device is provisioned with a unique cryptographic identity at the time of manufacturing, further ensures that only legitimate devices can connect to IoT networks.

Man-in-the-middle (MITM) attacks pose a significant risk to consumer IoT identity security. Attackers can intercept communication between IoT devices and cloud services, capturing authentication tokens, credentials, and sensitive data. Secure communication protocols, such as Transport Layer Security (TLS) and end-to-end encryption, protect IoT identity authentication from interception. Additionally, mutual authentication, where both the device and the network verify each other's identities before establishing a connection, can prevent unauthorized entities from hijacking communication sessions. Consumers should ensure that their IoT devices support encrypted communication protocols and avoid using unsecured public networks for device access.

Unauthorized access to consumer IoT devices often results from poor identity lifecycle management. Many users fail to update device credentials or revoke access when devices change ownership. This creates a risk where previous owners or unauthorized users may still have remote access to IoT devices, allowing them to exploit identity credentials for malicious purposes. Proper identity lifecycle management involves implementing automated credential expiration policies, requiring periodic password changes, and ensuring that device identities are reset when ownership changes. Manufacturers should also provide users with clear instructions on how to revoke device identities securely.

IoT device identity federation allows users to manage multiple devices under a unified authentication framework. With the growing number of consumer IoT devices in a household, managing individual credentials for each device becomes cumbersome. Federated identity management enables users to authenticate multiple devices using a single identity provider, simplifying access control. Standards such as OAuth and OpenID Connect allow IoT devices to authenticate through trusted third-party services, reducing the need for separate credentials for each device. However, federated identity solutions must be implemented securely to prevent unauthorized access, identity leaks, and single points of failure.

Behavioral authentication offers an additional layer of security for consumer IoT identities. Instead of relying solely on static credentials, behavioral authentication analyzes user interactions, including voice patterns, device usage habits, and movement characteristics, to continuously verify identity. AI-powered behavioral analytics can detect deviations in user behavior, flagging potential identity compromise attempts. For example, if a smart speaker suddenly starts responding to commands in an unfamiliar voice or a wearable fitness tracker exhibits movement patterns inconsistent with the owner, the system can trigger additional identity verification steps.

Identity security in consumer IoT devices must also address data privacy concerns. Many connected devices collect and transmit personal information, including location data, voice recordings, biometric data, and usage habits. If device identities are not securely managed, attackers can exploit identity credentials to gain unauthorized access to private user data. Privacy-preserving identity management techniques, such as anonymous authentication, zero-knowledge proofs, and decentralized identity models, help protect consumer identities while maintaining usability. Users should be given control over how their identity data is shared and stored, ensuring that personal information is not exposed to unnecessary risks.

AI-driven identity threat detection enhances security for consumer IoT devices by monitoring authentication attempts, device behaviors, and access patterns. Machine learning algorithms analyze real-time data to identify potential identity fraud, unauthorized access, and credential misuse. If an IoT device starts authenticating from an unusual location, accessing resources it has never interacted with before, or exhibiting other suspicious behaviors, AI-powered security systems can take automated actions, such as temporarily restricting access, sending security alerts, or requiring additional authentication factors. This proactive approach to identity security reduces the risk of compromised credentials being exploited.

Consumer IoT identity security must also comply with data protection regulations such as the General Data Protection Regulation (GDPR) and the California Consumer Privacy Act (CCPA). These regulations impose strict requirements on how identity-related data is collected, stored, and processed. Manufacturers and service providers must implement identity security best practices, including encrypted credential storage, access controls, and transparent identity management policies. Compliance with privacy regulations ensures that consumer IoT identity security is handled responsibly, reducing the risk of legal consequences and reputational damage.

As consumer IoT ecosystems continue to grow, identity security will play an increasingly critical role in ensuring safe and trustworthy interactions between users and devices. Implementing strong authentication mechanisms, securing device identities, encrypting communication, and leveraging AI-driven security analytics are essential steps in mitigating identity-related threats. Consumers must also take an active role in protecting their IoT device identities by using strong credentials, enabling security features, and staying informed about potential identity risks. A combination of technological advancements, regulatory frameworks, and user awareness will help create a more secure identity environment for consumer IoT devices.

IoT Identity and Compliance: GDPR, HIPAA, and NIST

The rapid expansion of the Internet of Things (IoT) has brought significant security and privacy concerns, particularly in the realm of identity management. As billions of connected devices collect, transmit, and process sensitive information, organizations must ensure that IoT identity management complies with regulatory frameworks designed to protect personal data and maintain cybersecurity standards. Regulations such as the General Data Protection Regulation (GDPR), the Health Insurance Portability and Accountability Act (HIPAA), and the National Institute of Standards and Technology (NIST) cybersecurity framework establish guidelines for managing IoT identities, securing authentication mechanisms, and preventing unauthorized access to sensitive data. Organizations deploying IoT solutions must align their identity management strategies with these regulations to mitigate security risks, protect user privacy, and ensure regulatory compliance.

GDPR, implemented by the European Union, is one of the most comprehensive data protection laws, setting strict guidelines for how organizations handle personal data, including identity-related information in IoT networks. Under GDPR, any IoT device that collects, processes, or transmits personally identifiable information (PII) must comply with data protection principles, including data minimization, lawful processing, and user consent. Identity security in IoT deployments must ensure that only authorized users and devices can access personal data while implementing encryption and access control mechanisms to prevent unauthorized identity disclosure. GDPR mandates that IoT devices incorporate privacy-by-design principles, meaning that identity protection must be integrated into device architecture from the outset rather than added as an afterthought.

One of the key challenges of GDPR compliance in IoT identity management is the principle of data subject rights, which grants individuals control over their personal information. IoT devices that store identity credentials or authentication logs must allow users to request access, correction, or deletion of their identity data. This presents a challenge for IoT deployments with distributed identity management systems, where identity-related data may be processed across multiple edge computing nodes, cloud services, and third-party platforms. To address GDPR requirements, organizations must implement transparent identity governance frameworks that provide users with visibility into how their identity data is collected, stored, and used. Encryption techniques such as pseudonymization and anonymization help protect IoT identity data while ensuring compliance with GDPR's data protection requirements.

HIPAA, a United States regulation designed to protect healthcare information, imposes strict identity security requirements for IoT devices used in medical environments. Many healthcare IoT devices, such as wearable health trackers, remote patient monitoring systems, and smart medical devices, collect and transmit protected health information (PHI). HIPAA mandates that healthcare organizations implement strong identity authentication mechanisms to ensure that only authorized users and devices can access PHI. Multi-factor authentication (MFA), biometric authentication, and role-based access control (RBAC) are essential for securing IoT identities in healthcare applications. IoT devices that interact with patient data must be capable of verifying identities securely while preventing unauthorized access to sensitive health records.

A significant challenge in HIPAA compliance for IoT identity management is ensuring the security of data transmission and storage. Healthcare IoT devices frequently communicate with cloud platforms, electronic health record (EHR) systems, and third-party medical applications. To prevent identity-related breaches, HIPAA requires that all transmitted and stored PHI be encrypted using strong cryptographic standards. IoT identity authentication mechanisms must enforce end-to-end encryption and implement secure key management to protect identity credentials from compromise. Organizations deploying IoT solutions in healthcare must also conduct regular identity security audits and risk assessments to ensure compliance with HIPAA security and privacy rules.

NIST provides cybersecurity guidelines that help organizations establish secure identity management practices for IoT devices. The NIST Cybersecurity Framework (NIST CSF) and NIST Special Publication 800-63 on digital identity offer best practices for implementing secure authentication, access control, and identity governance in IoT ecosystems. Unlike GDPR and HIPAA, which focus on regulatory compliance, NIST provides a structured approach to improving identity security in IoT networks, covering identity proofing, authentication assurance levels, and identity lifecycle management. Organizations following NIST guidelines must ensure that IoT devices support secure identity provisioning, use cryptographic authentication mechanisms, and implement continuous identity monitoring to detect anomalies and unauthorized access attempts.

NIST emphasizes the need for risk-based authentication in IoT environments, where authentication requirements are adjusted based on real-time security risks. For example, an IoT device performing routine operations within a secure environment may require minimal authentication, while a device attempting to access critical infrastructure systems may need stronger authentication, such as cryptographic certificates or hardware-based authentication tokens. This adaptive authentication approach aligns with Zero Trust security models, ensuring that IoT identities are continuously verified based on contextual security factors. NIST also highlights the importance of machine learning and artificial intelligence in identity threat detection, recommending the use of behavioral analytics to detect abnormal identity-related activities in IoT networks.

IoT identity compliance also requires organizations to implement secure credential storage and lifecycle management practices. Under GDPR, HIPAA, and NIST guidelines, identity credentials must be securely stored in tamper-resistant environments, such as hardware security modules (HSMs) or trusted execution environments (TEEs). Storing credentials in plaintext or hardcoding them into device firmware violates security best practices and increases the risk of identity breaches. Automated credential rotation and revocation policies help ensure that compromised credentials are not exploited indefinitely, while secure key management frameworks protect identity authentication keys from unauthorized access.

Regulatory compliance in IoT identity management extends beyond individual regulations, as many industries impose sector-specific identity security requirements. Financial institutions implementing IoT banking applications must comply with Payment Card Industry Data Security Standard (PCI DSS) guidelines for identity authentication. Smart cities deploying IoT-based identity solutions must align with public sector identity governance frameworks. Industrial IoT (IIoT) deployments must follow critical infrastructure protection standards, such as the IEC 62443 framework for securing industrial control systems. Organizations managing IoT identity security must ensure compliance with multiple overlapping regulations while maintaining strong authentication and privacy protection measures.

The convergence of AI-driven identity security and regulatory compliance is shaping the future of IoT identity management. AI-powered compliance monitoring tools analyze identity-related security logs, detect compliance violations, and generate automated reports to support regulatory audits. Machine learning models help organizations identify identity risks and enforce compliance policies dynamically, reducing the likelihood of regulatory penalties. AI-driven identity governance enhances transparency and accountability by providing real-time insights into IoT authentication trends, access control policies, and identity-related anomalies.

As IoT identity regulations evolve, organizations must adopt a proactive approach to compliance by implementing strong authentication, encryption, and identity monitoring practices. Compliance with GDPR, HIPAA, and NIST guidelines ensures that IoT identity security aligns with global cybersecurity and data protection standards. By integrating regulatory frameworks with AI-driven identity management, organizations can enhance security, protect user privacy, and establish trust in connected IoT ecosystems. Establishing a secure and compliant identity framework is essential for managing the risks associated with IoT identity authentication, ensuring that connected devices, applications, and users operate within a secure and regulated environment.

Identity Security in Smart Cities and Connected Infrastructure

The development of smart cities and connected infrastructure relies on the seamless integration of IoT devices, sensors, cloud platforms, and edge computing to improve urban efficiency, sustainability, and public safety. These systems enable real-time monitoring of traffic, energy consumption, public services, and environmental conditions, enhancing the quality of life for citizens. However, the interconnected nature of smart city infrastructure presents significant security challenges, particularly in managing the identities of devices, users, and applications that interact within these ecosystems. Identity security is crucial to preventing unauthorized access, ensuring data integrity, and protecting critical infrastructure from cyber threats.

One of the primary challenges in securing identities in smart cities is the vast scale and complexity of IoT deployments. Unlike traditional IT systems with centralized identity management, smart cities involve a decentralized network of connected devices that must authenticate dynamically across different domains. These include transportation systems, surveillance networks, emergency response units, smart grids, and connected healthcare services. Ensuring that each entity has a unique, verifiable identity is essential to preventing identity spoofing, unauthorized access, and data breaches. Implementing Public Key Infrastructure (PKI) helps establish trust by issuing digital certificates to IoT devices, enabling encrypted authentication and secure communication across smart city networks.

Device identity authentication is a fundamental aspect of smart city security, ensuring that only authorized sensors, cameras, and control systems can transmit data or interact with infrastructure components. Traditional identity management approaches relying on static credentials, such as hardcoded passwords, are inadequate for large-scale smart city environments. Dynamic identity authentication mechanisms, such as digital signatures and certificate-based authentication, allow devices to prove their legitimacy without relying on fixed credentials. Mutual authentication, where both the device and the network verify each other's identities before exchanging data, further strengthens security by preventing unauthorized devices from infiltrating smart city networks.

Identity federation is critical in smart city environments, where multiple government agencies, private entities, and service providers collaborate to manage infrastructure. Each entity may operate its own identity management system, making interoperability a key concern. Federated identity solutions allow different stakeholders to authenticate securely across multiple domains using a common identity framework. Standards such as OAuth, OpenID Connect, and Security Assertion Markup Language (SAML) enable cross-domain authentication while maintaining data privacy and access control. By adopting federated identity management, smart cities can facilitate seamless interactions between public services, utilities, and transportation systems without compromising security.

Biometric authentication plays an increasingly important role in smart city identity security, particularly in areas such as public transportation, law enforcement, and citizen services. Facial recognition, fingerprint scanning, and voice authentication provide convenient and secure methods for verifying identities without requiring physical credentials. However, biometric data must be protected against identity theft and unauthorized access. Privacy-preserving techniques such as biometric encryption, liveness detection, and decentralized storage help mitigate security risks while ensuring that personal identity information remains protected. AI-driven biometric authentication enhances security by analyzing behavioral patterns and detecting anomalies in real-time identity verification.

Access control in smart cities requires a dynamic and adaptive approach to identity security. Traditional role-based access control (RBAC) models may not be sufficient for large-scale connected infrastructure, where identity permissions must adjust based on real-time context. Attribute-Based Access Control (ABAC) allows smart city systems to make access decisions based on attributes such as location, device security status, time of access, and operational role. For example, an emergency response team may be granted temporary access to restricted infrastructure only during an active crisis, while a maintenance crew may require access to a smart grid substation based on verified work orders. Dynamic access control reduces the risk of unauthorized access while ensuring that identity permissions align with situational requirements.

Identity security in smart transportation systems is a key component of smart city infrastructure. Connected vehicles, traffic control systems, and public transportation networks rely on IoT-based identity authentication to ensure secure interactions between vehicles, infrastructure, and users. Vehicle-to-Everything (V2X) communication protocols enable connected vehicles to authenticate with traffic signals, toll systems, and emergency services. Implementing strong identity security measures, such as cryptographic authentication and secure key management, prevents identity spoofing attacks that could disrupt traffic operations or compromise passenger safety. Blockchain-based identity verification provides a decentralized approach to securing transportation identities, reducing the risk of unauthorized vehicle interactions.

Smart grids and energy infrastructure require robust identity security to prevent cyberattacks that could disrupt electricity distribution and critical services. Identity authentication mechanisms ensure that only authorized devices and users can access grid control systems, preventing attackers from manipulating power distribution. Multi-factor authentication (MFA), hardware-based authentication tokens, and secure firmware updates enhance the security of energy infrastructure identities. Continuous identity monitoring using AI-driven analytics detects unauthorized identity access attempts and abnormal device behaviors, allowing operators to respond proactively to potential security threats.

Public safety and law enforcement agencies rely on secure identity authentication to manage access to surveillance networks, emergency communication systems, and citizen services. IoT-connected surveillance cameras, body-worn sensors, and automated emergency response platforms must implement identity verification protocols to prevent unauthorized data access and ensure that only authorized personnel can control security systems. AI-powered identity analytics assist in detecting identity fraud, impersonation attempts, and unauthorized surveillance activities, strengthening overall smart city security.

Privacy is a major concern in smart city identity security, as IoT systems collect and process large amounts of personal data. Data protection regulations such as the General Data Protection Regulation (GDPR) and the California Consumer Privacy Act (CCPA) impose strict identity security requirements on smart city deployments. Privacy-preserving identity management techniques, such as zero-knowledge proofs, anonymous authentication, and decentralized identity frameworks, help balance security with individual privacy rights. Citizens must have control over how their identity data is used, with transparent identity policies and consent-based authentication mechanisms ensuring compliance with legal and ethical standards.

AI and machine learning enhance smart city identity security by automating threat detection, identity verification, and anomaly detection. AI-driven identity threat intelligence systems analyze authentication logs, device interactions, and network behaviors to identify suspicious activity. If an IoT sensor or smart infrastructure component exhibits unusual authentication patterns, AI-based security platforms can trigger automated responses, such as revoking identity credentials, isolating compromised devices, or escalating security alerts. Machine learning models continuously improve identity fraud detection capabilities, adapting to emerging threats in real time.

The future of smart city identity security will depend on a combination of strong authentication mechanisms, adaptive access control policies, AI-driven identity analytics, and decentralized identity frameworks. Secure identity management will be essential for ensuring the trustworthiness of smart infrastructure, preventing cyber threats, and protecting citizen privacy. As smart cities continue to evolve, governments, technology providers, and security professionals must collaborate to develop standardized identity security frameworks that support interoperability, scalability, and resilience. By implementing robust identity security strategies, smart cities can create safer, more efficient, and privacy-respecting digital environments for residents, businesses, and public services.

Secure Access Management for IoT Gateways

IoT gateways serve as critical intermediaries between edge devices, cloud platforms, and enterprise networks, facilitating communication, data aggregation, and security enforcement in IoT ecosystems. These gateways manage authentication, encryption, and data routing, ensuring that IoT devices operate securely while maintaining efficient connectivity. Because IoT gateways act as centralized points for device access and control, securing their identity and access management is essential to prevent unauthorized access, data breaches, and cyberattacks. Implementing robust secure access management for IoT gateways enhances device authentication, access control policies, and real-time monitoring, reducing the risk of identity-related threats and unauthorized operations.

One of the primary security concerns in IoT gateway access management is device authentication. IoT networks often include a vast array of connected devices, many of which lack native security capabilities. Weak authentication mechanisms, such as default credentials or static passwords, expose gateways to identity spoofing, unauthorized device enrollments, and credential-based attacks. To mitigate these risks, strong authentication protocols must be implemented to verify device identities before granting access to gateway resources. Public Key Infrastructure (PKI) enables certificate-based authentication, ensuring that only trusted devices can establish connections with IoT gateways. Each device is assigned a digital certificate, which is validated by the gateway before communication is allowed. This approach eliminates reliance on passwords and enhances identity trustworthiness across IoT deployments.

Multi-factor authentication (MFA) further strengthens access security by requiring multiple identity verification factors before allowing gateway access. Instead of relying solely on device credentials, MFA incorporates biometric authentication, one-time passcodes, or cryptographic tokens to ensure that only authorized users and devices gain access. This method prevents attackers from exploiting stolen credentials and enhances the overall security posture of IoT gateway access management. Additionally, identity federation mechanisms allow devices and users to authenticate across multiple gateways using a single set of credentials, reducing the complexity of managing access across distributed IoT networks.

Role-based access control (RBAC) and attribute-based access control (ABAC) provide structured access management policies for IoT gateways. RBAC assigns predefined roles to users, devices, and applications, ensuring that each entity has only the necessary permissions for its operations. Administrators, for example, may have full access to gateway configurations, while standard IoT devices may only have limited read-and-transmit permissions. ABAC enhances this approach by incorporating contextual attributes such as location, device type, security posture, and network conditions into access control decisions. Dynamic access management based on real-time factors allows gateways to enforce stricter policies when suspicious activity is detected, reducing the likelihood of unauthorized access.

IoT gateways must also support secure session management to prevent unauthorized access through session hijacking, replay attacks, or prolonged authentication sessions. Secure session tokens should be implemented to limit session durations and require re-authentication after a defined period. Time-sensitive authentication mechanisms, such as rotating cryptographic keys and expiring access tokens, further enhance session security by preventing unauthorized persistence. Gateways should enforce automatic session termination for inactive users and devices to mitigate risks associated with prolonged access.

Secure onboarding and provisioning of IoT devices are essential for preventing unauthorized access to gateways. When a new device is introduced into an IoT network, it must undergo an identity verification process before being granted access to gateway resources. Zero-touch provisioning (ZTP) automates secure onboarding by enabling devices to authenticate themselves using cryptographic keys and identity certificates. Secure boot mechanisms ensure that devices execute only trusted firmware, preventing tampering and identity spoofing. By integrating secure identity provisioning with access management policies, organizations can prevent unauthorized devices from infiltrating IoT gateway environments.

IoT gateways must implement secure remote access policies to prevent unauthorized administrative access. Many gateways allow remote configuration, monitoring, and software updates, increasing the risk of exploitation by attackers. Secure shell (SSH) access, virtual private network (VPN) tunnels, and Transport Layer Security (TLS) encryption must be enforced to protect remote connections from interception or unauthorized manipulation. Access logs should be continuously monitored to detect anomalous login attempts, unauthorized access requests, or potential identity compromise. AI-driven threat detection can analyze authentication patterns and flag suspicious access behavior in real time, allowing administrators to respond proactively to identity threats.

Logging and auditing play a crucial role in secure access management for IoT gateways. Comprehensive identity logs provide visibility into authentication events, access requests, and security policy enforcement. These logs help organizations track identity-related activities, detect policy violations, and conduct forensic investigations in the event of a security breach. Automated auditing tools can analyze identity access patterns and generate compliance reports for regulatory requirements such as GDPR, HIPAA, and NIST cybersecurity frameworks. By maintaining a clear record of access events, organizations can improve accountability and enhance security oversight.

Threat intelligence integration enhances IoT gateway access security by enabling real-time responses to emerging identity-based threats. AI-powered security platforms analyze threat intelligence feeds, identifying known attack vectors such as credential stuffing, identity spoofing, and brute-force authentication attempts. When a gateway detects an identity-related threat, it can automatically trigger response actions such as blocking access, revoking compromised credentials, or requiring additional authentication. Machine learning models continuously improve threat detection accuracy by adapting to new attack techniques and refining identity-based risk assessments.

IoT gateways also require secure firmware and software update mechanisms to protect access management systems from vulnerabilities. Unpatched gateway software can introduce security gaps that attackers exploit to bypass authentication controls. Secure update mechanisms, including cryptographically signed firmware and over-the-air (OTA) update verification, prevent unauthorized modifications to gateway identity systems. Automated patch management ensures that gateways remain protected against known security vulnerabilities, reducing the risk of identity compromise.

Regulatory compliance mandates strong identity security measures for IoT gateway access management. Compliance frameworks such as NIST SP 800-63, IEC 62443, and ISO 27001 outline best practices for identity authentication, access control, and credential security. Organizations deploying IoT gateways must align access management policies with regulatory standards to protect sensitive data, ensure secure authentication, and maintain legal compliance. Implementing industry-standard encryption, identity governance policies, and continuous security monitoring helps organizations meet compliance requirements while enhancing overall gateway security.

As IoT deployments expand, secure access management for gateways will remain a critical component of cybersecurity strategies. By implementing strong authentication mechanisms, dynamic access control policies, secure session management, and AI-driven threat detection, organizations can protect IoT gateways from identity-related threats. Ensuring that only authenticated devices, users, and applications can interact with gateways enhances security, prevents unauthorized access, and maintains the integrity of IoT ecosystems. Adopting best practices in secure access management enables organizations to safeguard IoT infrastructure while maintaining operational efficiency and compliance with security regulations.

Identity Security for 5G and IoT Networks

The integration of 5G technology with the Internet of Things (IoT) is transforming connectivity by enabling ultra-fast, low-latency communication and supporting massive machine-to-machine (M2M) interactions. 5G networks provide the scalability and efficiency required to connect billions of IoT devices across industries, including smart cities, healthcare, autonomous vehicles, and industrial automation. While 5G enhances IoT capabilities, it also introduces new identity security challenges. The decentralized nature of 5G networks, the increased number of connected devices, and the need for real-time authentication demand robust identity management strategies to prevent unauthorized access, identity spoofing, and cyber threats. Ensuring identity security in 5G-powered IoT networks requires a combination of strong authentication, dynamic access control, and AI-driven threat detection.

One of the key identity security challenges in 5G and IoT networks is managing the authentication of a massive number of connected devices. Unlike previous network generations, 5G supports billions of simultaneous connections, each requiring a unique and verifiable identity. Traditional authentication methods, such as static credentials or pre-shared keys, are insufficient for securing high-speed, high-density networks. To address this challenge, 5G networks implement the 3rd Generation Partnership Project (3GPP) Authentication and Key Agreement (AKA) protocol, which enables mutual authentication between devices and network infrastructure. The 5G-AKA protocol strengthens identity verification by using cryptographic techniques to prevent identity spoofing, ensuring that only authorized devices can connect to the network.

Public Key Infrastructure (PKI) plays a crucial role in 5G IoT identity security by providing certificate-based authentication for devices, users, and applications. Each IoT device is assigned a digital certificate, which is validated by a trusted certificate authority (CA) before establishing a network connection. This approach eliminates the risks associated with static credentials and ensures that all entities in a 5G IoT ecosystem can authenticate securely. Mutual authentication, where both the device and the network verify each other's identities, enhances trust and prevents unauthorized devices from gaining access to 5G infrastructure.

Zero Trust security principles are essential for managing identity security in 5G IoT networks. Traditional network security models assume that devices inside the network perimeter are trusted, increasing the risk of lateral movement attacks. Zero Trust enforces continuous identity verification, requiring every device, application, and user to authenticate before accessing network resources. Implementing Zero Trust in 5G-powered IoT environments involves using multi-factor authentication (MFA), dynamic access control, and continuous identity monitoring. By enforcing a least-privilege access model, Zero Trust ensures that devices and users only receive the permissions necessary for their specific functions, reducing the risk of identity-based attacks.

The deployment of network slicing in 5G introduces additional identity security challenges. Network slicing enables the creation of multiple virtualized network segments, each tailored to specific IoT applications. For example, a smart city might have separate network slices for traffic management, public safety, and energy distribution. Each network slice requires distinct identity authentication policies to ensure that devices accessing one slice cannot interfere with others. Implementing slice-specific identity controls, such as unique authentication credentials and access policies, prevents unauthorized cross-slice access and ensures the integrity of networked IoT services.

Identity federation enables seamless authentication across multiple 5G IoT networks and service providers. Many IoT applications operate across different network domains, requiring devices to authenticate with various service providers and cloud platforms. Federated identity management allows devices to authenticate once and access multiple services using a single identity, reducing authentication complexity and improving user experience. Protocols such as OAuth, OpenID Connect, and Security Assertion Markup Language (SAML) facilitate secure federated identity authentication while ensuring privacy and security. By adopting federated identity models, organizations can enhance interoperability between different 5G IoT ecosystems.

AI-driven identity threat detection enhances security in 5G IoT networks by continuously monitoring authentication patterns and identifying anomalies. Machine learning models analyze authentication logs, device behavior, and network traffic to detect suspicious activity that may indicate identity compromise. If an IoT device exhibits abnormal authentication attempts, such as multiple failed logins or accessing unauthorized network segments, AI-powered security systems can trigger automated responses, such as revoking credentials, blocking access, or requiring additional identity verification. AI-driven threat intelligence continuously improves identity security by adapting to emerging attack patterns and strengthening authentication policies.

Edge computing in 5G IoT networks introduces new identity management considerations. Many IoT applications process data at the edge to reduce latency and improve efficiency. Edge nodes, such as smart gateways and local processing units, require strong identity authentication to ensure that only authorized devices can communicate with them. Decentralized identity models, including blockchain-based identity verification, provide a tamper-proof method for managing edge device identities. By using blockchain's immutable ledger, IoT devices can securely register, verify, and authenticate their identities without relying on centralized identity providers. Blockchain-based identity solutions enhance trust in 5G IoT networks by eliminating single points of failure and ensuring transparent identity verification.

Secure access management in 5G IoT networks requires implementing dynamic identity and access control mechanisms. Unlike static access control models, dynamic access management continuously evaluates security risks and adjusts authentication policies in real-time. Identity attributes such as device location, security posture, time of access, and network behavior determine access permissions dynamically. Attribute-Based Access Control (ABAC) enables 5G IoT networks to enforce fine-grained access policies based on contextual identity factors. If a device attempts to access restricted resources from an unexpected location or exhibits suspicious authentication behavior, ABAC can automatically restrict or revoke access, preventing identity-based attacks.

Regulatory compliance plays a significant role in identity security for 5G IoT networks. Data protection laws such as the General Data Protection Regulation (GDPR) and the California Consumer Privacy Act (CCPA) impose strict identity management requirements on IoT deployments. Organizations must implement privacy-preserving identity authentication mechanisms, ensuring that user and device identities remain protected. Secure identity provisioning, encryption of identity credentials, and transparent identity policies help organizations comply with regulatory frameworks while maintaining strong security. Compliance with industry standards, such as the NIST Cybersecurity Framework and the GSMA IoT Security Guidelines, further strengthens identity security in 5G IoT networks.

Identity security in 5G and IoT networks requires a combination of strong authentication protocols, Zero Trust security models, AI-driven threat detection, and decentralized identity management. As the number of connected devices continues to grow, implementing scalable and secure identity solutions will be essential for preventing unauthorized access, protecting sensitive data, and ensuring the reliability of 5G-enabled IoT ecosystems. Organizations must adopt advanced identity security measures to address the evolving threats in high-speed, high-density networks, ensuring that connected devices, applications, and users operate within a secure and trusted environment.

Identity-Based Network Segmentation in IoT

As the Internet of Things (IoT) continues to expand, securing IoT networks becomes increasingly complex due to the sheer number and diversity of connected devices. Traditional network security models, which rely on perimeter-based defenses, are no longer sufficient to protect IoT ecosystems from sophisticated cyber threats. Identity-based network segmentation provides a more advanced security approach by dynamically enforcing network access policies based on the identities of devices, users, and applications. By segmenting networks based on identity attributes rather than static IP addresses or traditional VLANs, organizations can enhance security, reduce attack surfaces, and prevent lateral movement attacks.

One of the key challenges in IoT security is the heterogeneous nature of connected devices. IoT networks consist of various device types, ranging from sensors and industrial control systems to smart home appliances and autonomous vehicles. Many of these devices operate with different security capabilities, operating systems, and authentication mechanisms. Traditional network segmentation techniques, which rely on manual configurations and predefined IP ranges, struggle to accommodate the dynamic and diverse nature of IoT environments. Identity-based network segmentation solves this issue by assigning security policies based on unique device identities rather than static network attributes.

Identity-based segmentation relies on strong authentication mechanisms to verify the identities of devices before granting network access. Public Key Infrastructure (PKI) and digital certificates play a crucial role in establishing device identities within a segmented IoT network. Each device is provisioned with a cryptographic identity during manufacturing or onboarding, ensuring that only authenticated devices can access specific network segments. This approach prevents unauthorized devices from communicating with critical infrastructure and reduces the risk of identity spoofing attacks. Mutual authentication further strengthens security by requiring both devices and network controllers to verify each other's identities before exchanging data.

Zero Trust security principles align closely with identity-based network segmentation in IoT. Unlike traditional security models that assume trust based on network location, Zero Trust requires continuous identity verification and enforces access control policies at every interaction. In an IoT network segmented by identity, each device, user, or application must authenticate itself before gaining access to any network resource. Multi-factor authentication (MFA) and behavioral identity analytics further enhance security by verifying that devices and users exhibit normal authentication behaviors. If an IoT device deviates from expected behavior, access to certain network segments can be automatically restricted to mitigate potential threats.

Dynamic access control mechanisms enable identity-based segmentation to adapt to real-time security conditions. Unlike static segmentation, which relies on predefined firewall rules, identity-based segmentation continuously evaluates access requests based on contextual identity attributes. Attribute-Based Access Control (ABAC) allows organizations to define network policies based on factors such as device type, security posture, location, time of access, and operational role. For example, a connected surveillance camera may be granted access only to a specific video storage network segment but restricted from communicating with other IoT devices. If a security anomaly is detected, ABAC can automatically modify access permissions, limiting potential damage from compromised identities.

Micro-segmentation is a critical component of identity-based network segmentation in IoT. Traditional segmentation methods, such as

VLANs or subnetting, are often too broad to provide adequate security in complex IoT deployments. Micro-segmentation divides networks into smaller, tightly controlled segments, ensuring that devices and applications only communicate with authorized endpoints. Each segment enforces its own identity-based access policies, preventing attackers from moving laterally through the network if a device is compromised. Implementing software-defined networking (SDN) and network access control (NAC) solutions allows organizations to enforce micro-segmentation dynamically, reducing security risks without disrupting legitimate device operations.

Identity-based network segmentation also enhances security in industrial IoT (IIoT) environments, where operational technology (OT) systems must be protected from cyber threats. Industrial control systems, programmable logic controllers (PLCs), and smart sensors require strict access control policies to prevent unauthorized manipulation of critical processes. Segmentation by identity ensures that only verified devices and personnel can interact with sensitive industrial networks, reducing the risk of cyber-physical attacks. By implementing identity-aware firewalls and monitoring tools, organizations can detect and respond to unauthorized access attempts in real time.

AI-driven security analytics improve the effectiveness of identity-based segmentation by detecting identity-related anomalies and responding to emerging threats. Machine learning models analyze authentication logs, network traffic, and behavioral patterns to identify unusual activity that may indicate identity compromise. If an IoT device suddenly attempts to access a restricted network segment or exhibits unexpected authentication patterns, AI-powered security platforms can trigger automated segmentation adjustments. This adaptive security approach ensures that IoT networks remain resilient against identity-based attacks, minimizing the impact of compromised devices.

Secure identity provisioning is essential for maintaining the integrity of identity-based network segmentation. IoT devices must be securely enrolled into the network with verifiable identity credentials to prevent unauthorized access. Zero-touch provisioning (ZTP) automates the secure onboarding process, allowing devices to authenticate themselves without manual configuration. Blockchain-based identity management provides an additional layer of security by ensuring that device identities are immutable and tamper-proof. By decentralizing identity verification, blockchain enhances trust in IoT segmentation policies while eliminating reliance on centralized identity authorities.

Regulatory compliance frameworks emphasize the importance of identity-based network segmentation in securing IoT environments. Standards such as the NIST Cybersecurity Framework, IEC 62443 for industrial security, and GDPR for data protection mandate strict identity authentication and access control measures. Organizations must implement segmentation policies that align with compliance requirements, ensuring that IoT networks meet security and privacy standards. Automated identity governance solutions help enforce regulatory compliance by continuously monitoring access policies, auditing identity-based segmentation rules, and generating compliance reports.

Threat intelligence integration further strengthens identity-based segmentation by providing real-time insights into evolving cyber threats. By leveraging global threat intelligence feeds, IoT security platforms can detect identity-related attack patterns and proactively adjust segmentation policies. For example, if a known malware strain targets IoT devices with weak authentication, security systems can isolate affected network segments and block malicious traffic before it spreads. AI-powered threat intelligence continuously refines segmentation rules, ensuring that IoT networks remain protected against advanced cyber threats.

The adoption of 5G technology enhances the scalability and security of identity-based network segmentation in IoT. 5G networks support ultra-low latency and high-speed communication, enabling seamless authentication and enforcement of segmentation policies across distributed IoT ecosystems. Network slicing, a key feature of 5G, allows organizations to create isolated virtual network segments tailored to specific IoT applications. Each network slice enforces its own identity-based security policies, preventing unauthorized cross-slice access and enhancing overall IoT network resilience. By integrating 5G with identity-based segmentation, organizations can achieve a highly secure, flexible, and scalable IoT security architecture.

As IoT deployments continue to grow, identity-based network segmentation will play a vital role in securing connected environments. Implementing strong authentication mechanisms, dynamic access controls, micro-segmentation, and AI-driven threat detection ensures that IoT networks remain resilient against identity-based attacks. By leveraging identity-aware security frameworks, organizations can enhance network protection, prevent unauthorized access, and maintain the integrity of critical IoT infrastructure. Identity-based segmentation represents a fundamental shift in network security, providing a scalable and adaptive approach to managing access control in the evolving landscape of IoT connectivity.

Identity Security for Medical IoT Devices

The increasing adoption of medical Internet of Things (IoT) devices in healthcare has transformed patient monitoring, diagnostics, and treatment. Connected medical devices, such as wearable health monitors, insulin pumps, pacemakers, smart infusion pumps, and remote patient monitoring systems, enhance patient care by providing real-time health data to healthcare providers. However, the integration of these devices into healthcare networks introduces significant security risks, particularly in identity management. Ensuring the identity security of medical IoT devices is critical to protecting patient data, preventing unauthorized access, and maintaining the integrity of healthcare systems. Robust authentication, access control, and identity verification mechanisms are necessary to safeguard these life-critical devices from cyber threats.

One of the biggest challenges in securing medical IoT device identities is ensuring proper authentication while maintaining usability. Unlike traditional IT devices, medical IoT devices often operate in resource-constrained environments with limited processing power, memory, and battery life. Many medical devices were not originally designed with strong identity security in mind, leading to vulnerabilities such as weak authentication mechanisms, hardcoded credentials, and unencrypted identity data storage. To address these risks, medical IoT devices must implement strong authentication protocols, including digital certificates, public key infrastructure (PKI), and cryptographic identity verification. By assigning each device a unique cryptographic identity, healthcare organizations can ensure that only authenticated devices can access sensitive patient data and healthcare networks.

Multi-factor authentication (MFA) plays a crucial role in securing medical IoT identities. MFA requires devices and users to provide multiple forms of authentication before accessing medical data or device functions. A combination of biometric authentication, cryptographic tokens, and one-time passcodes enhances security by preventing unauthorized access, even if login credentials are compromised. Implementing MFA ensures that only authorized healthcare personnel, patients, or administrators can interact with medical IoT devices, reducing the risk of identity-based attacks.

Device identity spoofing is a significant threat to medical IoT security, where attackers impersonate legitimate medical devices to intercept sensitive health data or manipulate device functions. If an attacker successfully spoofs the identity of a connected medical device, they could gain unauthorized access to hospital networks, alter treatment protocols, or interfere with real-time patient monitoring. Implementing certificate-based authentication and mutual authentication protocols helps prevent identity spoofing by requiring devices to verify each other's identities before exchanging data. Medical IoT devices must also support secure boot mechanisms, ensuring that only authorized and tamper-proof firmware is executed during startup.

Medical IoT networks require dynamic identity and access control mechanisms to regulate how devices interact with healthcare systems. Role-based access control (RBAC) and attribute-based access control (ABAC) frameworks allow healthcare providers to define strict identity-based access policies. For example, an IoT-enabled glucose monitor should only transmit data to a patient's electronic health record (EHR) system and authorized healthcare providers while preventing unauthorized applications or users from accessing sensitive information. Implementing access control policies based on device identity attributes, user roles, and contextual factors ensures that medical IoT devices operate securely within a controlled healthcare environment.

The use of biometric identity authentication in medical IoT enhances security and usability. Many wearable health devices and smart medical sensors incorporate fingerprint recognition, facial recognition, or voice authentication to verify patient identities. This prevents unauthorized use of medical devices and ensures that patient-specific data remains secure. AI-driven behavioral authentication further strengthens security by continuously analyzing user interaction patterns and detecting anomalies that may indicate identity compromise. If a medical IoT device detects unusual user behavior, such as an unexpected authentication location or abnormal device usage, it can trigger additional security verification steps or restrict access.

Data privacy is a critical concern in medical IoT identity security, as healthcare devices handle highly sensitive patient information. Regulations such as the Health Insurance Portability and Accountability Act (HIPAA) in the United States and the General Data Protection Regulation (GDPR) in the European Union impose strict requirements on how medical IoT devices manage identity data. Medical IoT identity management must align with these regulatory frameworks by ensuring that patient identity data is encrypted, access is restricted to authorized entities, and identity logs are securely maintained for auditing purposes. Privacy-preserving identity techniques, such as zero-knowledge proofs and anonymization, enable medical IoT devices to authenticate securely while minimizing the exposure of personally identifiable information (PII).

AI-driven identity threat detection plays an important role in monitoring medical IoT networks for suspicious activity. Machine learning algorithms analyze authentication patterns, device behavior, and network traffic to detect potential identity-related attacks. If an AI-powered security system identifies abnormal authentication attempts, such as repeated failed login attempts on a medical device or unauthorized remote access requests, it can trigger automated responses, including revoking credentials, isolating compromised devices, or notifying security teams. AI-enhanced identity security helps healthcare organizations proactively respond to emerging threats and minimize the risk of cyberattacks targeting medical IoT devices.

Secure identity provisioning ensures that medical IoT devices are enrolled into healthcare networks without exposing them to identity-related vulnerabilities. Zero-touch provisioning (ZTP) automates the secure onboarding of medical devices, allowing them to register with healthcare systems without requiring manual configuration. Blockchain-based identity verification enhances the security of medical IoT identity management by providing a decentralized and tamper-proof method for verifying device identities. By eliminating reliance on centralized identity providers, blockchain-based identity frameworks enhance trust and security in medical IoT networks.

Medical IoT device manufacturers must implement secure firmware update mechanisms to prevent attackers from exploiting identity-related vulnerabilities in outdated software. Over-the-air (OTA) updates with cryptographic signature verification ensure that only authorized updates are installed on medical devices. Regular identity security audits, penetration testing, and compliance assessments help healthcare organizations evaluate the effectiveness of their identity management policies and ensure that medical IoT devices remain secure.

Identity federation enhances interoperability in medical IoT networks by enabling secure cross-domain authentication between healthcare providers, cloud platforms, and medical device manufacturers. Federated identity management allows patients and healthcare professionals to access multiple medical IoT systems using a single identity, reducing authentication complexity while maintaining security. Secure identity delegation mechanisms ensure that authorized caregivers and family members can securely access medical devices without exposing patient credentials to unauthorized entities.

As medical IoT ecosystems continue to expand, ensuring strong identity security will be essential to protecting patient safety, securing sensitive health data, and preventing cyber threats. By implementing robust authentication mechanisms, dynamic access control, AI-driven identity monitoring, and regulatory compliance frameworks, healthcare organizations can mitigate the risks associated with medical IoT identity security. A comprehensive approach to identity protection ensures that connected medical devices remain trustworthy, resilient, and secure within modern healthcare environments.

Identity in Vehicle-to-Everything (V2X) Communication

Vehicle-to-Everything (V2X) communication is a fundamental technology driving the future of intelligent transportation systems, enabling vehicles to communicate with infrastructure, pedestrians, cloud services, and other vehicles in real time. By facilitating high-speed, low-latency communication between road users and traffic management systems, V2X enhances road safety, reduces congestion, and improves overall driving efficiency. However, the security and trustworthiness of V2X networks heavily depend on identity management. Secure identity authentication ensures that only legitimate vehicles, roadside units, and control systems can participate in V2X communication, preventing unauthorized access, identity spoofing, and malicious interference.

One of the primary challenges in securing identities in V2X communication is the need for real-time authentication while maintaining low latency. Vehicles exchanging safety-critical information must authenticate each other within milliseconds to avoid communication delays that could impact decision-making on the road. Traditional identity verification methods, such as username-password authentication or centralized identity databases, are impractical in high-speed, mobile environments. Instead, V2X identity security relies on cryptographic authentication mechanisms, including digital certificates and public key infrastructure (PKI), to establish trusted communication channels without introducing significant latency.

Public Key Infrastructure (PKI) plays a critical role in V2X identity management by enabling certificate-based authentication for vehicles, infrastructure nodes, and road users. Each vehicle is issued a digital certificate by a trusted certificate authority (CA), ensuring that it can authenticate itself before transmitting messages to other vehicles or traffic systems. When a vehicle sends a safety-related message, such as a collision warning or lane change alert, receiving vehicles verify the sender's identity by validating the attached digital certificate. This process prevents attackers from injecting false messages into V2X networks and ensures that only authenticated entities participate in vehicle communication.

Mutual authentication further strengthens V2X identity security by requiring both communicating entities to verify each other's identities before exchanging information. When a vehicle communicates with a smart traffic light or pedestrian detection system, both parties must authenticate their digital certificates to establish a secure communication session. Mutual authentication ensures that rogue or compromised devices cannot impersonate trusted V2X participants, reducing the risk of identity spoofing attacks.

One of the unique aspects of V2X identity security is the need for pseudonymization to balance privacy and authentication. Unlike traditional network authentication, where a persistent identity is associated with a device or user, V2X communication must protect driver privacy by preventing long-term tracking. Pseudonym-based identity management allows vehicles to periodically change their digital certificates, ensuring that no single certificate is continuously linked to a specific vehicle. Certificate rotation mechanisms, known as pseudonym certificates, prevent malicious actors from tracking vehicle movements while maintaining the integrity of V2X authentication.

Identity-based access control ensures that only authorized entities can access specific V2X communication channels. Roadside infrastructure, such as traffic signals and toll booths, must authenticate vehicles before granting access to restricted services or data. Role-based access control (RBAC) allows V2X networks to enforce policies based on the identity and permissions of each entity. For example, emergency response vehicles may have higher priority in traffic management systems, allowing them to override traffic signals, while civilian vehicles must adhere to standard traffic control rules. Attribute-Based Access Control (ABAC) extends this approach by incorporating real-time contextual factors, such as vehicle speed, location, and network conditions, to dynamically adjust access permissions.

The rise of 5G networks has introduced new opportunities for improving V2X identity security. With ultra-low latency and high-speed connectivity, 5G enables real-time authentication and identity verification for massive numbers of connected vehicles. 5G network slicing allows transportation agencies to create dedicated V2X communication channels with strict identity security policies, isolating vehicle authentication from other network traffic. Secure Identity

Management in 5G-V2X environments ensures that vehicles can authenticate with multiple service providers, cloud platforms, and traffic management systems without compromising security.

Blockchain technology enhances V2X identity security by providing decentralized, tamper-proof identity verification. Instead of relying on a single certificate authority, blockchain-based identity management enables vehicles and infrastructure nodes to authenticate each other using a distributed ledger. Each identity transaction, including certificate issuance, revocation, and authentication logs, is recorded on an immutable blockchain ledger, preventing unauthorized identity modifications. Blockchain-based identity frameworks also improve interoperability across different V2X service providers by providing a standardized trust model for vehicle authentication.

AI-powered identity threat detection strengthens V2X security by analyzing authentication patterns and detecting anomalies in real time. Machine learning algorithms monitor V2X identity authentication events, identifying suspicious behavior such as repeated authentication failures, certificate forgery attempts, or unauthorized access to V2X communication channels. If an AI-driven identity monitoring system detects an anomaly, it can automatically revoke compromised certificates, block unauthorized entities, or trigger security alerts for further investigation. AI-driven analytics improve V2X network resilience by continuously adapting to evolving identity-based cyber threats.

Identity lifecycle management in V2X networks ensures that digital certificates remain secure throughout their operational lifespan. Vehicles must undergo secure onboarding processes to receive identity credentials from trusted authorities, and certificate renewal and revocation mechanisms must be in place to prevent outdated or compromised identities from being exploited. Automatic certificate expiration and reissuance policies help maintain V2X identity security by ensuring that authentication credentials remain up-to-date and resistant to long-term attacks.

Regulatory compliance plays a crucial role in defining identity security standards for V2X communication. Governments and transportation agencies enforce cybersecurity frameworks, such as the National

Institute of Standards and Technology (NIST) guidelines and the European Union's Cooperative Intelligent Transport Systems (C-ITS) regulations, to mandate secure identity management in connected vehicle networks. Compliance with these regulations ensures that V2X identity security aligns with global best practices for authentication, privacy protection, and secure communication.

Vehicle-to-Everything communication will continue to evolve as autonomous vehicles, smart transportation infrastructure, and advanced AI-driven traffic management systems become more prevalent. Ensuring secure identity authentication in V2X networks is essential for building trust in intelligent transportation systems, preventing cyberattacks, and protecting road users. By implementing PKI-based authentication, pseudonymized identity management, AI-driven threat detection, and decentralized identity frameworks, V2X ecosystems can achieve a high level of security while maintaining privacy and efficiency. Secure identity management in V2X communication will be critical in shaping the future of connected and autonomous mobility, enabling safer and more intelligent transportation systems worldwide.

Managing Identity in Large-Scale IoT Deployments

The rapid expansion of the Internet of Things (IoT) has introduced complex identity management challenges, particularly in large-scale deployments where thousands or even millions of connected devices must be authenticated, authorized, and managed securely. In smart cities, industrial automation, healthcare, and smart grid infrastructures, IoT devices continuously exchange data and interact with critical systems, requiring a robust identity framework to prevent unauthorized access and maintain security. Managing identity in large-scale IoT deployments requires a combination of secure authentication, automated provisioning, scalable access control, and continuous identity monitoring to ensure that all devices operate within a trusted environment.

One of the primary challenges in large-scale IoT identity management is device authentication. Unlike traditional IT environments, where authentication is primarily user-based, IoT networks must authenticate devices, gateways, and applications. Static credentials such as hardcoded passwords or pre-shared keys are impractical in large-scale deployments due to the risk of credential reuse, manual mismanagement, and security vulnerabilities. Instead, modern IoT identity frameworks rely on cryptographic authentication methods, including digital certificates and Public Key Infrastructure (PKI), to ensure that each device has a unique and verifiable identity. PKI-based authentication allows IoT devices to securely authenticate with network services, cloud platforms, and edge computing nodes without relying on weak or reusable credentials.

Automated identity provisioning is critical for large-scale IoT deployments, as manual onboarding processes become inefficient and error-prone when managing thousands of devices. Zero-touch provisioning (ZTP) enables IoT devices to authenticate and enroll themselves securely into a network without requiring human intervention. During ZTP, devices generate cryptographic keys, request digital certificates from a trusted certificate authority (CA), and establish secure connections with management platforms. This automated identity provisioning process eliminates the need for manual configuration, reducing deployment time while enhancing security. Secure identity provisioning mechanisms ensure that only authorized devices can join an IoT network, preventing rogue or counterfeit devices from gaining access.

Scalability is a key concern when implementing identity management in large IoT ecosystems. Traditional identity and access management (IAM) systems designed for enterprise IT environments struggle to scale efficiently in IoT networks, where millions of identities must be managed simultaneously. Federated identity management provides a scalable solution by enabling multiple identity providers to authenticate devices across different domains. By using protocols such as OAuth, OpenID Connect, and Security Assertion Markup Language (SAML), federated identity systems allow IoT devices to authenticate once and securely access multiple services without requiring separate credentials for each system. This approach simplifies identity management while ensuring interoperability between cloud platforms, edge computing nodes, and IoT service providers.

Role-based access control (RBAC) and attribute-based access control (ABAC) are essential for enforcing identity-based security policies in large-scale IoT environments. RBAC assigns permissions based on predefined roles, ensuring that IoT devices only have access to resources necessary for their operation. For example, a smart thermostat may be allowed to communicate with a home automation system but restricted from accessing security camera feeds. ABAC enhances this approach by incorporating real-time contextual factors such as device location, network conditions, and operational status into access control decisions. By implementing dynamic access control mechanisms, organizations can ensure that IoT devices operate within defined security parameters while minimizing the risk of unauthorized access.

Identity lifecycle management plays a crucial role in maintaining security across the lifespan of IoT devices. Unlike traditional IT assets, IoT devices often have long operational lifespans, requiring secure identity management from deployment to decommissioning. Identity lifecycle processes include initial provisioning, credential renewal, access revocation, and secure device retirement. Automated identity lifecycle management ensures that device identities remain valid and up to date while preventing unauthorized access from obsolete or compromised devices. Secure decommissioning processes revoke authentication credentials and remove device identities from the network when devices reach end-of-life, preventing attackers from exploiting abandoned IoT assets.

Blockchain technology offers an innovative approach to identity management in large-scale IoT deployments by providing decentralized, tamper-proof identity verification. Traditional identity management models rely on centralized authorities, which can become bottlenecks or single points of failure in high-scale environments. Blockchain-based identity management eliminates the need for a central identity provider by distributing identity verification across a secure ledger. Each IoT device is assigned a verifiable identity on the blockchain, allowing it to authenticate with other devices and services without relying on intermediaries. Blockchain-based identity solutions enhance security, improve transparency, and reduce the risk of identity fraud in IoT networks.

AI-driven identity analytics improve security in large-scale IoT deployments by continuously monitoring authentication patterns, detecting anomalies, and responding to potential identity threats. Machine learning models analyze historical authentication data to identify deviations from normal behavior, flagging suspicious identity activities such as repeated failed authentication attempts, credential misuse, or unauthorized access requests. AI-powered identity threat detection enables organizations to respond proactively to identity-based attacks, automatically revoking compromised credentials or enforcing additional authentication requirements for high-risk devices. Integrating AI into IoT identity management enhances security while reducing the administrative burden associated with manual identity monitoring.

Regulatory compliance is a major consideration for identity security in large-scale IoT deployments, as organizations must ensure that identity management practices align with industry regulations and data protection laws. Compliance frameworks such as the General Data Protection Regulation (GDPR), the California Consumer Privacy Act (CCPA), and the National Institute of Standards and Technology (NIST) Cybersecurity Framework impose strict requirements on identity authentication, access control, and data privacy. Organizations must implement strong encryption, access logging, and audit mechanisms to ensure compliance while protecting IoT identities from unauthorized access. Automated compliance reporting tools help organizations monitor identity security policies and generate audit logs for regulatory review.

Identity-based network segmentation strengthens security in large-scale IoT deployments by isolating devices into secure network zones based on their identity attributes. Traditional network segmentation relies on static IP-based policies, which become difficult to manage in large, dynamic IoT environments. Identity-based segmentation enforces access policies based on device roles, authentication levels, and operational contexts. For example, industrial IoT sensors monitoring factory equipment may be segmented into a dedicated network zone with restricted access to external systems, while medical IoT devices transmitting patient data may require additional authentication before accessing cloud services. Implementing identity-aware segmentation reduces attack surfaces and prevents unauthorized lateral movement within IoT networks.

As IoT ecosystems continue to expand, managing identity in large-scale deployments will require a combination of automation, cryptographic authentication, federated identity management, and AI-driven security analytics. Organizations must adopt scalable identity solutions that provide seamless authentication, enforce dynamic access control policies, and ensure compliance with regulatory requirements. By implementing advanced identity management frameworks, organizations can secure large-scale IoT deployments, prevent unauthorized access, and maintain the trustworthiness of connected devices. Strengthening identity security in IoT networks will be essential for enabling the next generation of smart cities, industrial automation, and connected healthcare systems while ensuring the resilience and integrity of digital infrastructure.

Secure Identity APIs for IoT and Edge Services

The rapid adoption of IoT and edge computing has created a need for secure identity management solutions that facilitate authentication, authorization, and access control across distributed environments. Application Programming Interfaces (APIs) play a crucial role in enabling identity services for IoT and edge computing by providing standardized methods for identity verification, credential management, and access enforcement. Secure Identity APIs allow devices, applications, and users to interact with authentication systems while ensuring that identity data remains protected from unauthorized access and cyber threats. Proper implementation of secure identity APIs in IoT and edge services is essential for maintaining trust, reducing security risks, and ensuring compliance with identity protection regulations.

One of the main challenges in securing identity APIs for IoT and edge services is the highly distributed nature of these environments. Unlike traditional enterprise systems where authentication and identity management are centralized, IoT and edge computing involve a vast number of connected devices operating in decentralized networks.

Identity APIs must provide scalable authentication mechanisms that support millions of connected devices while maintaining low latency and high availability. The use of lightweight authentication protocols such as OAuth 2.0, OpenID Connect, and JSON Web Tokens (JWT) ensures that identity APIs can efficiently authenticate devices without introducing excessive computational overhead.

Authentication APIs provide the foundation for securing IoT and edge services by verifying the identities of devices, applications, and users before granting access to resources. These APIs issue authentication tokens that serve as digital credentials, allowing entities to prove their identity without transmitting sensitive authentication details repeatedly. Multi-factor authentication (MFA) can be integrated into authentication APIs to enhance security by requiring additional identity verification steps. For example, an IoT device attempting to access an edge service may need to provide a cryptographic signature or biometric verification in addition to its API key. This multi-layered approach prevents unauthorized devices from gaining access through compromised credentials.

Authorization APIs enforce access control policies by determining which IoT devices and users are permitted to perform specific actions within an edge computing environment. Role-Based Access Control (RBAC) and Attribute-Based Access Control (ABAC) are commonly used to define authorization rules that identity APIs enforce dynamically. In RBAC, devices and users are assigned roles with predefined permissions, such as read-only access for sensors and full administrative privileges for edge gateways. ABAC enhances authorization policies by incorporating contextual attributes such as device location, network security status, and operational behavior. Secure Identity APIs must support real-time policy evaluation to ensure that access control decisions adapt to changing security conditions.

Identity federation APIs enable seamless authentication across multiple IoT and edge platforms by allowing devices and users to authenticate once and access various services without re-entering credentials. Federated identity management is particularly useful in hybrid environments where IoT devices interact with cloud services, enterprise networks, and third-party applications. Secure Identity APIs facilitate single sign-on (SSO) authentication, reducing authentication complexity while maintaining strong security controls. Implementing standards such as Security Assertion Markup Language (SAML) and OAuth 2.0 for federated authentication ensures interoperability across different identity providers and service ecosystems.

The security of Identity APIs depends on robust cryptographic mechanisms that protect authentication data from interception and tampering. Transport Layer Security (TLS) encryption must be enforced for all API communications to prevent man-in-the-middle (MITM) attacks. Mutual TLS (mTLS) authentication enhances security by requiring both the client and the API server to verify each other's identities before exchanging identity-related data. Digital signatures and hashed authentication tokens further protect identity API transactions by ensuring the integrity of transmitted credentials. Secure storage of API keys, access tokens, and cryptographic credentials is essential to prevent unauthorized access to identity management functions.

Rate limiting and anomaly detection mechanisms help prevent identity API abuse and credential-based attacks. API security frameworks must implement rate-limiting policies to restrict the number of authentication requests a device or application can make within a specific time frame. This mitigates brute-force attacks, credential stuffing, and denial-of-service (DoS) attempts targeting authentication endpoints. AI-driven anomaly detection enhances API security by identifying unusual authentication patterns, such as repeated login failures, rapid credential changes, or access attempts from unauthorized regions. When suspicious activity is detected, the identity API can trigger additional security measures, such as enforcing stricter authentication requirements or blocking access requests.

Decentralized identity solutions enhance security in IoT and edge computing by reducing reliance on centralized identity providers. Blockchain-based identity APIs allow IoT devices to authenticate using decentralized identifiers (DIDs), eliminating single points of failure and improving resilience against identity fraud. Verifiable credentials stored on blockchain networks enable devices to prove their identities without relying on a central authentication authority. Secure Identity APIs that support decentralized identity frameworks provide greater flexibility, privacy, and transparency in identity management while reducing the risks associated with traditional credential storage methods.

Secure identity lifecycle management is a critical function of Identity APIs in IoT and edge services. Devices must undergo secure onboarding processes where they receive unique identity credentials that establish trust with the network. API-based identity provisioning automates this process, enabling devices to self-register with authentication servers while adhering to strict identity verification requirements. Once operational, IoT devices require periodic identity credential updates, key rotations, and access policy adjustments to maintain security. Secure decommissioning APIs ensure that devices that reach end-of-life have their identity credentials revoked to prevent unauthorized access after they are retired.

Regulatory compliance requirements must be integrated into Secure Identity APIs to protect sensitive identity data and ensure adherence to global security standards. Regulations such as the General Data Protection Regulation (GDPR), the California Consumer Privacy Act (CCPA), and the National Institute of Standards and Technology (NIST) cybersecurity guidelines impose strict security measures for identity authentication and access control. Identity APIs must support data encryption, role-based authorization, audit logging, and user consent mechanisms to meet compliance requirements. Providing API-based access to compliance reports and security audits enables organizations to demonstrate adherence to regulatory frameworks while maintaining strong identity security.

AI-powered identity governance enhances the security of Identity APIs by automating identity risk assessments and enforcing security policies based on real-time analytics. Machine learning models analyze API authentication logs, device behaviors, and access requests to detect potential identity threats. If an API-based authentication system detects an anomaly, such as an IoT device attempting to authenticate from an untrusted location, it can dynamically adjust access control policies, enforce additional verification steps, or revoke compromised credentials. AI-driven security automation reduces manual administrative overhead while improving the accuracy and efficiency of identity protection.

As IoT and edge computing environments continue to grow, the role of Secure Identity APIs will become increasingly important in protecting authentication and access control functions. Implementing cryptographically secure authentication, enforcing robust authorization policies, integrating AI-driven threat detection, and supporting decentralized identity management will enable organizations to build resilient identity security frameworks. By leveraging secure and scalable Identity APIs, organizations can ensure the integrity of IoT and edge services while mitigating identity-related cyber threats. Strengthening API-based identity security will be essential for enabling trust, interoperability, and regulatory compliance in modern connected ecosystems.

The Future of Decentralized Identity in IoT

The rapid expansion of the Internet of Things (IoT) has highlighted the need for robust identity management solutions that can support billions of interconnected devices while ensuring security, privacy, and interoperability. Traditional identity management models rely on centralized authentication authorities that control identity verification and access management. However, as IoT networks grow in complexity, centralized identity systems become impractical due to scalability issues, security vulnerabilities, and the risk of single points of failure. Decentralized identity (DID) is emerging as a transformative solution that eliminates reliance on central identity providers and enables devices to establish and manage their own identities securely. The future of decentralized identity in IoT will be driven by blockchain technology, self-sovereign identity (SSI), cryptographic authentication, and AI-powered identity governance.

Decentralized identity shifts control over digital identities from centralized entities to individuals and devices, ensuring greater autonomy, privacy, and security. Unlike traditional identity models, where identity credentials are stored in centralized databases managed by service providers, decentralized identity frameworks allow IoT devices to generate and manage their own identities using cryptographic techniques. Decentralized identifiers (DIDs) replace static credentials, such as usernames and passwords, with blockchain-based identity records that are verifiable, tamper-proof, and resistant to identity theft. DIDs allow devices to authenticate securely without relying on third-party identity providers, reducing the risk of identity compromise and unauthorized access.

Blockchain technology plays a crucial role in enabling decentralized identity for IoT by providing a transparent, immutable, and distributed ledger for identity verification. Each IoT device can register its DID on a blockchain network, allowing other devices and services to verify its identity without needing to query a centralized database. Smart contracts automate identity validation and access control, ensuring that only authorized entities can interact within IoT ecosystems. The decentralized nature of blockchain eliminates the need for a single trusted authority, reducing the risk of identity fraud, credential breaches, and unauthorized data access.

Self-sovereign identity (SSI) enhances decentralized identity by allowing IoT devices to own and control their identity credentials without relying on intermediaries. In an SSI framework, devices generate cryptographic key pairs and store verifiable identity attributes on a distributed ledger. When authentication is required, an IoT device presents a cryptographic proof of its identity without exposing sensitive identity data. This privacy-preserving authentication method ensures that devices can securely communicate with networks, cloud services, and edge computing platforms while maintaining control over their identity attributes. SSI also enables selective disclosure, allowing devices to share only the necessary identity information required for authentication, reducing the risk of identity tracking and profiling.

The interoperability of decentralized identity frameworks is essential for enabling seamless authentication across multiple IoT platforms and service providers. Current identity management systems are often siloed, requiring devices to maintain separate credentials for different services, cloud platforms, and network operators. Decentralized identity standards, such as the World Wide Web Consortium (W3C) Decentralized Identifiers (DID) specification and the Verifiable Credentials (VC) model, provide a unified approach to IoT identity management. By adopting these standards, organizations can ensure that IoT devices can authenticate across different ecosystems without requiring redundant identity credentials.

The integration of AI and machine learning in decentralized identity management enhances security by enabling real-time threat detection, anomaly detection, and adaptive authentication. AI-driven identity analytics monitor IoT authentication patterns and detect irregularities that may indicate identity compromise. If an IoT device exhibits unusual authentication behavior, such as repeated failed login attempts, unexpected geolocation changes, or interactions with unauthorized services, AI-based identity governance systems can trigger automated responses. These responses may include enforcing additional authentication factors, revoking compromised credentials, or blocking suspicious access attempts. AI-enhanced decentralized identity management strengthens IoT security by continuously adapting to evolving identity threats.

Decentralized identity also enhances identity lifecycle management for IoT devices, ensuring secure onboarding, authentication, and decommissioning. Secure identity provisioning allows new IoT devices to generate and register their own decentralized identities upon joining a network, eliminating manual configuration and reducing human intervention. Throughout the device lifecycle, identity credentials can be updated, rotated, and revoked securely without requiring centralized identity authorities. When a device reaches the end of its operational life, its decentralized identity can be deactivated using cryptographic revocation mechanisms, ensuring that decommissioned devices do not pose security risks.

One of the biggest advantages of decentralized identity in IoT is improved privacy protection. Traditional identity management models require devices to share personal and device-specific information with centralized authentication servers, increasing the risk of identity tracking and data misuse. With decentralized identity, IoT devices retain full control over their identity attributes and can authenticate without exposing sensitive data. Privacy-enhancing technologies such as zero-knowledge proofs (ZKPs) enable IoT devices to prove their identity without revealing underlying identity details. By reducing the amount of personally identifiable information (PII) shared during authentication, decentralized identity frameworks enhance user privacy while maintaining strong security.

Regulatory compliance is an important consideration in the future of decentralized identity in IoT. Data protection laws such as the General Data Protection Regulation (GDPR) and the California Consumer Privacy Act (CCPA) impose strict requirements on how identity data is collected, stored, and processed. Decentralized identity aligns with these regulations by providing a privacy-first approach that gives users and devices control over their identity information. Organizations deploying IoT solutions must ensure that their decentralized identity implementations comply with regulatory standards by enforcing encryption, consent-based authentication, and transparent identity governance policies.

The adoption of decentralized identity in IoT will depend on industry-wide collaboration and standardization efforts. Governments, technology providers, and regulatory bodies must work together to establish common frameworks that support decentralized identity authentication across different sectors. Emerging decentralized identity initiatives, such as the Decentralized Identity Foundation (DIF) and the Trust Over IP (ToIP) Foundation, aim to create interoperable identity solutions that work across IoT ecosystems. As these standards gain traction, organizations will be able to deploy decentralized identity frameworks at scale, ensuring that IoT networks remain secure, efficient, and privacy-respecting.

The transition to decentralized identity in IoT represents a fundamental shift in how digital identities are managed, authenticated, and secured. By eliminating reliance on centralized identity authorities, enhancing privacy, and enabling cryptographic authentication, decentralized identity frameworks provide a scalable and resilient solution for IoT security. As blockchain, AI, and self-sovereign identity technologies continue to evolve, decentralized identity will become the foundation for trust and security in IoT ecosystems. Organizations must embrace decentralized identity strategies to secure their IoT deployments, protect user privacy, and enable the next generation of connected devices to operate in a secure and autonomous manner.

Identity Security in Smart Homes and Connected Devices

The rapid adoption of smart home technology has introduced a wide range of connected devices that enhance convenience, efficiency, and security. Smart speakers, thermostats, security cameras, door locks, and home automation hubs provide seamless control over residential environments while integrating with cloud services, mobile applications, and voice assistants. However, the increasing number of interconnected devices in smart homes also presents significant security challenges, particularly in identity management. Identity security in smart homes ensures that only authorized users and devices can access and control connected systems, preventing unauthorized access, identity spoofing, and data breaches. A strong identity framework is essential for maintaining trust in smart home ecosystems and protecting the privacy of homeowners.

One of the biggest risks in smart home identity security is weak authentication mechanisms. Many smart home devices still rely on default credentials, weak passwords, or static authentication tokens, making them vulnerable to brute-force attacks and credential stuffing. Attackers often exploit these vulnerabilities to gain unauthorized access, manipulate device settings, or use compromised devices as entry points into home networks. Implementing strong authentication methods, such as cryptographic certificates, biometric authentication, and multi-factor authentication (MFA), significantly improves identity security. MFA requires users to verify their identity using multiple factors, such as a password combined with a one-time passcode sent to a mobile device, reducing the risk of unauthorized access.

Device identity management plays a crucial role in ensuring that only trusted smart home devices are allowed to communicate within a home network. Each device must have a unique and verifiable identity that can be authenticated before being granted access to networked resources. Public Key Infrastructure (PKI) enables certificate-based authentication, ensuring that smart home devices can verify each other's identities using cryptographic keys. Secure device provisioning during the manufacturing and onboarding process ensures that only legitimate devices receive identity credentials. This prevents unauthorized or counterfeit devices from infiltrating smart home networks and impersonating trusted devices.

One of the most significant challenges in smart home identity security is preventing identity spoofing attacks, where an attacker impersonates a legitimate device to gain access to sensitive data or system controls. If a smart door lock or security camera is spoofed, attackers could bypass authentication mechanisms and gain physical or digital access to a home. Implementing mutual authentication, where both the device and the network verify each other's identities before establishing communication, mitigates the risk of identity spoofing. Secure communication protocols, such as Transport Layer Security (TLS) and mutual TLS (mTLS), ensure that authentication data cannot be intercepted or manipulated during transmission.

Access control is another critical component of identity security in smart home environments. Role-Based Access Control (RBAC) allows homeowners to define access levels for different users, ensuring that only authorized individuals can control specific devices. For example, parents may have full administrative access to all smart home systems, while children may have limited access to lighting controls but no control over security settings. Attribute-Based Access Control (ABAC) extends access management by incorporating contextual factors, such as time of access, device location, and user behavior. If an unauthorized user attempts to control a smart device from an unusual location, ABAC can trigger additional authentication steps or block access entirely.

Biometric authentication enhances identity security in smart homes by enabling secure and frictionless user authentication. Smart home devices equipped with fingerprint scanners, facial recognition, or voice authentication provide stronger security than traditional password-based authentication. AI-powered behavioral biometrics further improve security by continuously analyzing user interactions, detecting anomalies in voice patterns, touch gestures, or device usage habits. If a smart home system detects an unusual authentication attempt, it can prompt additional verification methods to confirm the user's identity.

Identity security in smart home environments must also address data privacy concerns. Many connected devices collect and process sensitive personal data, including voice recordings, video footage, and behavioral analytics. Unauthorized access to smart home identity data can lead to privacy violations, identity theft, or targeted cyberattacks. Privacy-preserving identity management techniques, such as decentralized identity frameworks, zero-knowledge proofs, and anonymization, reduce the risk of data exposure. Decentralized identity models allow users to maintain control over their identity credentials, ensuring that authentication processes do not rely on centralized identity providers that could be vulnerable to breaches.

AI-driven identity threat detection enhances security by monitoring authentication attempts, access requests, and device behaviors in real time. Machine learning models analyze identity-related activity patterns, identifying potential identity compromise events, unauthorized access attempts, or unusual authentication behaviors. If an AI-based identity monitoring system detects a suspicious authentication request, such as an attempt to access a smart home network from an untrusted location, it can take immediate action by revoking credentials, requiring additional authentication, or alerting the homeowner. AI-driven security analytics improve the detection of identity-based threats, reducing the likelihood of successful identity attacks.

Smart home identity security must also incorporate secure identity lifecycle management practices to ensure that devices maintain strong security throughout their operational lifespan. When adding new devices to a smart home network, secure identity provisioning ensures that only verified devices receive authentication credentials. Periodic credential updates and key rotations help prevent identity compromise due to outdated authentication mechanisms. When devices are retired or replaced, identity credentials must be securely revoked to prevent unauthorized reuse. Automated identity lifecycle management systems help maintain secure authentication processes without requiring constant manual intervention.

Regulatory compliance is an important consideration for identity security in smart home ecosystems. Data protection laws such as the General Data Protection Regulation (GDPR) and the California

Consumer Privacy Act (CCPA) impose strict requirements on how smart home identity data is managed. Smart home manufacturers and service providers must ensure that authentication mechanisms comply with privacy regulations by implementing encryption, consent-based authentication, and transparent identity governance policies. Users should have control over their identity data, with the ability to manage access permissions, revoke device credentials, and monitor authentication logs to ensure security.

The integration of blockchain technology into smart home identity security provides an additional layer of protection by enabling tamper-proof identity verification. Blockchain-based identity management allows devices to register and authenticate their identities on a decentralized ledger, eliminating the risk of centralized identity breaches. Smart contracts can automate identity verification and access control, ensuring that only authorized devices and users can interact within a smart home network. Blockchain enhances trust and transparency in smart home identity security by providing an immutable record of identity transactions.

As smart home ecosystems continue to evolve, identity security will remain a critical factor in protecting connected devices and user privacy. By implementing strong authentication mechanisms, mutual device verification, AI-driven threat detection, and decentralized identity management, smart home environments can mitigate identity-related risks. Homeowners and manufacturers must prioritize identity security to prevent unauthorized access, identity spoofing, and data breaches. Strengthening identity security in smart homes ensures that connected devices remain trustworthy, secure, and resilient against emerging cyber threats.

Quantum-Safe Identity Security for IoT

The rise of quantum computing poses a significant threat to traditional cryptographic security, including identity authentication and access control in the Internet of Things (IoT). Current identity security mechanisms rely heavily on public key cryptography, including RSA, ECC, and other asymmetric encryption techniques, which quantum computers could potentially break using advanced algorithms such as Shor's algorithm. As quantum computing capabilities advance, IoT identity security must evolve to withstand quantum attacks and ensure that authentication mechanisms remain secure against future threats. Quantum-safe identity security involves developing and implementing cryptographic techniques that can resist quantum decryption, ensuring the continued protection of IoT identity authentication and key management.

One of the primary challenges in securing IoT identities against quantum threats is the longevity of IoT devices. Many IoT devices are designed to function for years or even decades, making them susceptible to future quantum attacks if they rely on vulnerable encryption standards. A compromised identity authentication system could allow attackers to impersonate legitimate devices, intercept sensitive data, or manipulate IoT infrastructure. Transitioning to quantum-safe cryptographic methods is essential for ensuring that long-term IoT deployments remain resilient against emerging quantum threats.

Post-quantum cryptography (PQC) is the leading approach to securing IoT identities against quantum attacks. PQC algorithms are designed to be resistant to quantum decryption while remaining compatible with existing digital infrastructure. The National Institute of Standards and Technology (NIST) is in the process of standardizing quantum-safe cryptographic algorithms, including lattice-based, code-based, hash-based, and multivariate polynomial-based encryption schemes. Lattice-based cryptography, in particular, shows promise for IoT applications due to its efficiency and resistance to quantum computing attacks. Integrating PQC into IoT identity security ensures that devices can authenticate securely even as quantum computing capabilities expand.

Quantum key distribution (QKD) provides another quantum-resistant approach to securing IoT identities. Unlike traditional cryptographic techniques, which rely on mathematical complexity, QKD uses the principles of quantum mechanics to ensure secure key exchange. In QKD, encryption keys are transmitted using quantum particles, such as photons, which cannot be measured or intercepted without altering their state. This guarantees that any attempt to eavesdrop on the key exchange process is immediately detectable, making QKD an ideal solution for securing IoT identity authentication. However, QKD requires specialized quantum communication infrastructure, which may not be feasible for all IoT deployments.

One of the biggest challenges in implementing quantum-safe identity security in IoT is ensuring that cryptographic transitions do not disrupt existing authentication mechanisms. Many IoT devices rely on embedded cryptographic hardware, such as Trusted Platform Modules (TPMs) and Hardware Security Modules (HSMs), which are optimized for traditional encryption standards. Upgrading these devices to support post-quantum cryptographic algorithms requires careful planning to avoid compatibility issues and maintain security during the transition period. Hybrid cryptographic solutions, which combine classical and quantum-safe encryption, offer a practical approach by allowing IoT devices to gradually migrate to quantum-resistant authentication while maintaining backward compatibility.

Device identity authentication in IoT must incorporate quantum-safe digital signatures to prevent unauthorized access and identity forgery. Traditional digital signature algorithms, such as RSA and ECDSA, will become vulnerable to quantum attacks, potentially allowing attackers to forge signatures and impersonate legitimate IoT devices. Quantum-safe alternatives, such as hash-based signatures and lattice-based signatures, provide a secure alternative by ensuring that digital identities cannot be compromised by quantum decryption techniques. Implementing quantum-safe digital signatures in IoT identity management ensures that device authentication remains trustworthy, even in a post-quantum computing environment.

Quantum-safe identity security must also address secure key management and distribution. In IoT environments, cryptographic keys are used for authentication, secure communication, and access control. If these keys are compromised by quantum attacks, IoT devices become vulnerable to identity spoofing and data interception. Quantum-safe key exchange mechanisms, such as lattice-based key encapsulation and quantum-resistant Diffie-Hellman protocols, ensure that identity authentication keys remain protected against quantum decryption. Implementing post-quantum key management solutions helps IoT devices maintain secure identity authentication while mitigating future quantum security risks.

Zero Trust security principles align with quantum-safe identity security by enforcing continuous authentication and access verification. In a Zero Trust model, IoT devices must prove their identity at every interaction, regardless of their network location. Quantum-safe authentication methods ensure that devices cannot be impersonated or compromised through quantum attacks. Implementing identity-based micro-segmentation further enhances security by isolating IoT devices into controlled network environments, preventing compromised identities from accessing critical systems. Combining Zero Trust with quantum-resistant identity security ensures that IoT deployments remain secure even as quantum computing capabilities evolve.

AI-driven identity security enhances quantum-safe authentication by continuously monitoring identity interactions for anomalies. Machine learning models analyze authentication patterns and detect suspicious activity, such as unauthorized identity access attempts or deviations from normal authentication behavior. AI-powered security platforms can dynamically adjust authentication policies, enforce additional verification steps, or revoke compromised credentials in response to detected threats. By integrating AI-driven identity monitoring with quantum-safe cryptographic techniques, IoT identity security can remain adaptive and resilient against emerging cyber threats.

Regulatory compliance plays a crucial role in ensuring the adoption of quantum-safe identity security for IoT. Governments and cybersecurity agencies are actively developing guidelines for post-quantum cryptographic transitions, requiring organizations to adopt quantum-resistant authentication mechanisms to protect sensitive data. Regulations such as NIST's Post-Quantum Cryptography Standardization, the European Union Agency for Cybersecurity (ENISA) recommendations, and emerging IoT security frameworks emphasize the need for future-proof identity authentication solutions. Organizations deploying IoT solutions must align with these regulatory requirements to ensure compliance while mitigating the risks associated with quantum computing advancements.

Decentralized identity frameworks provide an additional layer of security by reducing reliance on centralized authentication authorities. Blockchain-based identity management enables IoT devices to register and authenticate their identities using distributed ledgers, ensuring that identity credentials remain secure and tamper-proof. Quantum-safe cryptographic techniques can be integrated into blockchain identity frameworks to protect identity authentication from quantum decryption. By combining decentralized identity management with quantum-resistant encryption, IoT deployments can achieve higher levels of security, transparency, and trust.

Future IoT security architectures must integrate quantum-safe identity authentication at every layer, from device identity provisioning to secure key management and real-time authentication monitoring. Organizations must begin the transition to quantum-resistant identity security now to ensure that IoT networks remain protected as quantum computing capabilities advance. Hybrid cryptographic approaches, AI-driven security analytics, and decentralized identity frameworks will play a key role in enabling secure and resilient IoT identity authentication. By proactively adopting quantum-safe identity security, organizations can safeguard IoT ecosystems against the threats of tomorrow while maintaining trust, interoperability, and compliance in the evolving cybersecurity landscape.

Digital Twins and Identity Security in IoT

The concept of digital twins has revolutionized the way organizations manage, monitor, and optimize IoT ecosystems. A digital twin is a virtual representation of a physical device, system, or process that continuously receives real-time data from its physical counterpart. By using advanced analytics, artificial intelligence, and IoT connectivity, digital twins help predict failures, improve operational efficiency, and enable remote management of physical assets. However, as digital twins become more integrated into IoT networks, ensuring their identity security becomes critical. Unauthorized access, identity spoofing, and data manipulation can compromise digital twins, leading to security risks in physical systems. Strong identity security measures are essential to protect both digital twins and their corresponding physical devices.

One of the main challenges in securing digital twins is ensuring that their identity remains verifiable and tamper-proof. Each digital twin must be uniquely linked to its physical counterpart, preventing attackers from forging or manipulating identity credentials. Traditional identity authentication methods, such as static credentials or simple API keys, are not sufficient for securing digital twins in complex IoT environments. Instead, cryptographic authentication mechanisms, such as Public Key Infrastructure (PKI) and blockchain-based identity verification, provide a more secure approach to ensuring that digital twins and physical devices maintain a trusted relationship. By using cryptographic certificates, digital twins can authenticate themselves before accessing network resources, preventing unauthorized clones or impersonations.

Mutual authentication between digital twins and physical devices is critical to maintaining identity security. In a secure IoT ecosystem, the physical device must verify the authenticity of its digital twin before transmitting data, and the digital twin must also verify that it is communicating with the correct physical device. Implementing mutual authentication protocols, such as Transport Layer Security (TLS) or mutual TLS (mTLS), ensures that only authorized digital twins can interact with their corresponding devices. This prevents attackers from intercepting or manipulating data exchanges, reducing the risk of identity fraud in digital twin systems.

Access control plays a crucial role in protecting digital twins from unauthorized interactions. Role-Based Access Control (RBAC) and Attribute-Based Access Control (ABAC) allow organizations to define strict policies on who or what can access digital twins. RBAC assigns predefined permissions based on user roles, ensuring that only authorized personnel can modify digital twin configurations or retrieve sensitive data. ABAC further enhances security by incorporating contextual identity attributes, such as time, location, device status, and network security conditions, into access control decisions. If a digital twin attempts to access a restricted system from an untrusted location or device, the system can automatically deny access or require additional authentication.

Digital twins require continuous identity monitoring to detect anomalies that may indicate identity compromise or unauthorized access attempts. AI-driven identity security systems analyze authentication logs, access patterns, and behavioral data to identify suspicious activities. If an AI-powered monitoring system detects an unusual authentication attempt, such as a digital twin accessing unauthorized network segments or transmitting unexpected data, it can trigger automated security responses. These responses may include revoking credentials, isolating compromised digital twins, or notifying security teams of potential identity threats. AI-enhanced security analytics provide a proactive defense against identity-related attacks targeting digital twin systems.

Blockchain technology enhances digital twin identity security by providing decentralized identity verification. Traditional identity management systems rely on central authorities to authenticate digital twins, creating single points of failure that can be exploited by attackers. Blockchain-based identity frameworks store digital twin identity credentials on a distributed ledger, ensuring that authentication records remain immutable and tamper-proof. By using smart contracts, organizations can automate identity validation, allowing digital twins to authenticate securely without relying on a centralized identity provider. Blockchain-based identity management improves transparency, interoperability, and trust in digital twin ecosystems.

Digital twins in industrial IoT (IIoT) environments require strict identity security to prevent cyber-physical attacks. In sectors such as manufacturing, energy, and critical infrastructure, digital twins control complex systems, including smart factories, power grids, and transportation networks. If an attacker gains access to a digital twin, they can manipulate its data, causing operational disruptions or even physical damage. Implementing zero-trust security principles ensures that digital twins are continuously verified before being granted access to industrial control systems. Enforcing real-time authentication, micro-segmentation, and continuous monitoring helps protect IIoT digital twins from identity-based cyber threats.

Regulatory compliance is an essential aspect of digital twin identity security, as industries must adhere to strict cybersecurity standards and data protection laws. Regulations such as the General Data Protection Regulation (GDPR), the California Consumer Privacy Act (CCPA), and the National Institute of Standards and Technology (NIST) cybersecurity guidelines require organizations to implement strong authentication and access control measures. Digital twin identity management must align with these regulations by ensuring that identity credentials are encrypted, access policies are enforced, and authentication logs are securely maintained for compliance audits. Organizations that fail to protect digital twin identities may face legal and financial consequences due to data breaches or regulatory violations.

Digital twin identity lifecycle management ensures that digital twins maintain secure identities throughout their operational lifespan. When a digital twin is created, it must undergo a secure onboarding process, where it receives verifiable identity credentials. As digital twins interact with IoT networks, their identity credentials may require periodic updates or rotations to prevent long-term exposure to security vulnerabilities. When a digital twin is retired or replaced, its identity credentials must be securely revoked to prevent unauthorized reuse. Automated identity lifecycle management streamlines these processes, ensuring that digital twins remain protected against identity compromise.

Quantum-safe identity security is an emerging consideration for digital twins, as quantum computing advances may threaten traditional cryptographic authentication mechanisms. Post-quantum cryptographic algorithms provide a long-term security solution for digital twin identity management, ensuring that authentication processes remain resilient against quantum attacks. Quantum-safe digital signatures, key exchange mechanisms, and identity authentication frameworks will play a crucial role in securing digital twins against future cybersecurity threats. Organizations deploying digital twins must consider quantum-resistant cryptographic transitions to maintain identity security in an era of evolving cyber risks.

The future of digital twin identity security will be shaped by advancements in AI-driven identity analytics, decentralized authentication, and quantum-safe cryptographic techniques. Organizations must implement robust authentication, access control, and continuous monitoring mechanisms to protect digital twins from identity threats. As digital twins become an integral part of IoT ecosystems, securing their identities will be critical to ensuring trust, efficiency, and resilience in connected environments. By adopting strong identity security measures, organizations can safeguard digital twin systems, prevent unauthorized access, and maintain the integrity of real-world and virtual IoT interactions.

Identity Security for IoT Supply Chain Management

The integration of IoT devices in supply chain management has transformed logistics, manufacturing, and inventory tracking by providing real-time data on shipments, warehouse conditions, and operational efficiency. IoT-enabled supply chains rely on interconnected devices such as RFID tags, GPS trackers, smart sensors, and automated robotic systems to streamline operations and improve visibility. However, the growing number of connected devices introduces significant identity security risks, as unauthorized access, identity spoofing, and supply chain attacks can compromise critical operations. Securing identity authentication and access control in IoT supply chain environments is essential to ensuring trust, preventing cyber threats, and maintaining the integrity of global logistics networks.

One of the biggest challenges in securing IoT identities in supply chain management is authenticating a vast number of interconnected devices operating across multiple stakeholders. Unlike traditional IT environments where authentication is limited to enterprise users and servers, IoT supply chains involve multiple manufacturers, logistics providers, warehouses, distributors, and retailers, each with their own connected devices. Ensuring that each IoT device has a unique, verifiable identity prevents malicious actors from injecting counterfeit devices or manipulating supply chain data. Public Key Infrastructure (PKI) provides a scalable authentication solution by issuing digital certificates to IoT devices, ensuring that only verified entities can access supply chain systems.

Unauthorized access to supply chain IoT networks can result in data manipulation, product counterfeiting, and operational disruptions. Identity spoofing, where attackers impersonate legitimate devices, is a significant risk that can lead to fraudulent transactions or misrouted shipments. Implementing strong identity verification protocols, such as digital signatures and cryptographic authentication, ensures that IoT devices cannot be cloned or manipulated. Mutual authentication between supply chain entities prevents unauthorized devices from interacting with logistics platforms, ensuring that data exchanges occur only between trusted parties.

IoT supply chain identity security must also address secure onboarding and provisioning of devices. As new sensors, tracking devices, and automated systems are introduced into supply chain networks, they must be securely registered and authenticated before accessing logistics systems. Zero-touch provisioning (ZTP) automates secure device onboarding by enabling IoT devices to enroll themselves with identity credentials issued by a trusted certificate authority. By eliminating manual configuration processes, ZTP reduces the risk of identity mismanagement and ensures that all connected devices are securely authenticated from the moment they join the supply chain network.

Access control in IoT supply chain management requires granular identity-based policies to regulate which devices and users can interact with logistics platforms. Role-Based Access Control (RBAC) allows organizations to assign predefined roles to supply chain entities, ensuring that each device has only the necessary permissions required for its function. For example, RFID tags tracking shipments should be granted read-only access to supply chain data, while warehouse robotics may require write permissions to update inventory records. Attribute-Based Access Control (ABAC) enhances this model by incorporating real-time contextual factors such as device location, operational status, and security posture into access control decisions.

Blockchain technology enhances identity security in IoT supply chain management by providing decentralized authentication and tamper-proof identity records. Traditional identity management models rely on centralized authentication servers, which can become single points of failure in global supply chain networks. Blockchain-based identity verification ensures that each IoT device is registered on a distributed ledger, allowing stakeholders to verify device identities without relying on a central authority. Smart contracts automate identity validation and access control, ensuring that only authenticated devices and users can execute supply chain transactions. Blockchain's immutability prevents attackers from modifying identity records, reducing the risk of identity fraud and counterfeit device infiltration.

AI-driven identity security plays a crucial role in monitoring authentication activities and detecting suspicious behavior in IoT supply chain networks. Machine learning models analyze authentication patterns, access logs, and device interactions to identify anomalies that may indicate identity compromise. If an AI-powered identity monitoring system detects unusual behavior, such as an IoT tracking device accessing unauthorized data or an RFID tag exhibiting abnormal communication patterns, it can trigger automated security responses. These responses may include revoking compromised credentials, enforcing additional authentication requirements, or isolating suspicious devices from the supply chain network.

Identity federation improves interoperability in IoT supply chain ecosystems by enabling seamless authentication across multiple logistics providers, cloud platforms, and third-party vendors. Supply chains often involve multiple organizations operating across different network environments, requiring devices to authenticate with various service providers. Federated identity management allows IoT devices to authenticate once and securely interact with multiple supply chain entities using a common identity framework. Standards such as OAuth, OpenID Connect, and Security Assertion Markup Language (SAML) facilitate federated authentication, reducing authentication complexity while ensuring strong identity security.

Secure identity lifecycle management ensures that IoT supply chain devices maintain strong authentication throughout their operational lifespan. Identity credentials must be periodically updated, rotated, and revoked to prevent long-term exposure to security risks. Automated credential renewal policies ensure that IoT devices do not continue using outdated authentication methods, reducing the risk of identity compromise. When devices reach end-of-life, secure decommissioning processes revoke identity credentials, ensuring that retired devices cannot be exploited by attackers. Identity lifecycle management reduces the risk of unauthorized access by ensuring that only active, authenticated devices can interact with supply chain systems.

Regulatory compliance is a critical factor in IoT supply chain identity security, as global supply chains must adhere to strict data protection and cybersecurity regulations. Standards such as the General Data Protection Regulation (GDPR), the National Institute of Standards and Technology (NIST) Cybersecurity Framework, and the Internet of Things Cybersecurity Improvement Act mandate strong authentication, encryption, and access control measures for IoT devices. Organizations must implement identity security policies that align with these regulations to protect sensitive supply chain data and ensure compliance with international security requirements. Secure logging, audit trails, and encryption of identity-related transactions help supply chain organizations meet regulatory obligations while maintaining strong identity security.

Quantum-safe identity security is an emerging concern for IoT supply chain authentication, as quantum computing advancements may render traditional cryptographic methods obsolete. Post-quantum cryptographic algorithms ensure that supply chain identity authentication remains resilient against quantum decryption threats. Quantum-safe digital signatures and key exchange protocols provide long-term protection for identity credentials, preventing attackers from using quantum computers to break authentication mechanisms. Organizations managing IoT supply chains must prepare for the transition to quantum-resistant cryptographic standards to future-proof their identity security frameworks.

The future of identity security in IoT supply chain management will be shaped by advancements in AI-driven identity analytics, decentralized authentication, and post-quantum cryptographic techniques. Organizations must implement robust authentication mechanisms, access control policies, and continuous identity monitoring to protect supply chain networks from identity-based threats. By adopting blockchain-based identity verification, federated authentication, and quantum-safe cryptographic solutions, supply chain organizations can enhance security, prevent counterfeit device infiltration, and ensure the integrity of global logistics operations. Strengthening identity security in IoT supply chains is essential for building a secure, transparent, and resilient logistics infrastructure that can withstand evolving cyber threats.

Identity and Data Sovereignty in IoT Networks

As the Internet of Things (IoT) continues to expand across industries, managing identity security and ensuring data sovereignty have become critical concerns. IoT networks generate vast amounts of data that must be authenticated, stored, and transmitted securely while complying with local and international regulations. Identity management in IoT is closely linked to data sovereignty, as organizations must ensure that only authorized entities can access, modify, or transfer data across connected devices and cloud services. The challenge lies in maintaining strong identity authentication while enforcing data residency and governance requirements that vary by region and industry.

Data sovereignty refers to the principle that data is subject to the laws and regulations of the country where it is collected or stored. In IoT networks, data sovereignty becomes complex because devices operate across different jurisdictions, transmitting data between cloud providers, edge computing environments, and international service providers. Identity security plays a key role in maintaining data sovereignty by ensuring that only authenticated users, devices, and applications can access specific data based on regulatory requirements. If identity authentication mechanisms fail to enforce sovereignty rules, sensitive IoT data may be transferred or accessed in unauthorized locations, leading to compliance violations and security risks.

One of the primary challenges in IoT identity management is ensuring that identity authentication aligns with data sovereignty policies. Traditional identity and access management (IAM) systems often rely on centralized authentication services, which may store user credentials and identity-related metadata in foreign jurisdictions. This creates potential legal and regulatory concerns, as organizations must ensure that identity data does not violate sovereignty laws. Decentralized identity frameworks, such as self-sovereign identity (SSI) and blockchain-based authentication, provide an alternative by allowing IoT devices and users to manage their own identity credentials without relying on a central authority. By using decentralized identity verification, organizations can enforce data sovereignty while maintaining strong authentication and access control.

Public Key Infrastructure (PKI) is a fundamental component of IoT identity security, enabling devices to authenticate themselves using cryptographic certificates. In the context of data sovereignty, PKI-based identity authentication ensures that only authorized devices can access data within specific regions or jurisdictions. When an IoT device attempts to transmit data across borders, the receiving system can verify the device's digital certificate to determine whether it complies with regional sovereignty requirements. Certificate-based authentication also prevents identity spoofing, ensuring that attackers cannot impersonate legitimate devices to gain access to sovereign data.

Role-Based Access Control (RBAC) and Attribute-Based Access Control (ABAC) provide granular identity management policies that align with data sovereignty requirements. RBAC assigns predefined roles to devices and users, ensuring that only authorized entities can access or transfer data within specific jurisdictions. ABAC enhances access control by incorporating real-time contextual attributes, such as device location, time of access, and network security posture, into identity verification decisions. If an IoT device attempts to transfer data outside an authorized jurisdiction, ABAC policies can automatically block the request or require additional identity verification before proceeding.

Data encryption plays a crucial role in enforcing data sovereignty while maintaining identity security. Encrypting IoT data at rest and in transit ensures that even if data is transmitted across borders, unauthorized entities cannot access its contents without proper decryption keys. End-to-end encryption (E2EE) enables secure identity authentication while ensuring that data remains protected throughout its lifecycle. In sovereign cloud environments, organizations can implement encryption key management policies that restrict access to cryptographic keys based on regional compliance requirements. By enforcing strict encryption policies tied to identity authentication, organizations can maintain control over IoT data sovereignty while preventing unauthorized access.

Federated identity management enhances data sovereignty in IoT by enabling seamless authentication across multiple cloud providers and regional infrastructures while ensuring compliance with local regulations. Federated identity systems allow IoT devices to authenticate with multiple service providers using a single identity, reducing the need for separate identity credentials for different jurisdictions. However, federated authentication must be carefully implemented to ensure that identity metadata and authentication logs do not violate data sovereignty laws. Privacy-enhancing identity protocols, such as anonymous authentication and zero-knowledge proofs, enable devices to authenticate without exposing identity data to unauthorized jurisdictions, preserving both security and compliance.

Blockchain-based identity security provides a decentralized approach to enforcing data sovereignty while maintaining trust in IoT authentication. By storing identity credentials on an immutable distributed ledger, blockchain ensures that identity verification remains transparent and tamper-proof while reducing reliance on centralized authentication authorities. Smart contracts automate identity validation and access control, ensuring that IoT devices can authenticate securely without transmitting sensitive identity data across unauthorized jurisdictions. Blockchain's decentralized nature aligns with data sovereignty requirements by allowing organizations to enforce regional authentication policies without relying on external identity providers that may operate in foreign jurisdictions.

AI-driven identity security enhances compliance with data sovereignty regulations by continuously monitoring authentication patterns and detecting anomalies in identity access requests. Machine learning algorithms analyze identity logs, network behaviors, and authentication attempts to identify potential violations of sovereignty policies. If an IoT device exhibits unusual authentication behavior, such as accessing data from an unauthorized jurisdiction or attempting to bypass access control policies, AI-driven security platforms can trigger automated responses, including revoking credentials, enforcing additional authentication factors, or blocking unauthorized data transfers. AI-based security analytics help organizations proactively enforce identity sovereignty while reducing the risk of compliance breaches.

Regulatory compliance frameworks play a crucial role in shaping identity security policies for IoT data sovereignty. Laws such as the General Data Protection Regulation (GDPR) in Europe, the California Consumer Privacy Act (CCPA), and China's Cybersecurity Law impose strict data localization requirements, mandating that organizations store and process identity-related data within specific jurisdictions. IoT identity management systems must align with these regulations by implementing sovereignty-aware authentication policies, ensuring that identity credentials are stored and accessed in compliance with regional laws. Compliance reporting tools help organizations track identity access events, generate audit logs, and demonstrate adherence to sovereignty requirements.

The emergence of quantum computing poses future challenges for IoT identity security and data sovereignty. Traditional cryptographic identity authentication methods, including RSA and ECC, may become vulnerable to quantum decryption attacks, potentially compromising sovereign authentication systems. Post-quantum cryptographic algorithms, such as lattice-based encryption and hash-based signatures, provide quantum-resistant authentication mechanisms that ensure long-term identity security. Organizations must prepare for the transition to quantum-safe identity authentication to maintain compliance with data sovereignty regulations while mitigating the risk of quantum-based cyber threats.

Identity security and data sovereignty in IoT networks require a combination of strong authentication mechanisms, decentralized identity frameworks, encryption policies, and AI-driven monitoring. Organizations must implement identity governance strategies that enforce sovereignty-aware authentication, prevent unauthorized data transfers, and ensure compliance with international data protection laws. By adopting blockchain-based authentication, quantum-resistant cryptographic techniques, and federated identity management, IoT ecosystems can maintain secure and sovereign identity authentication while adapting to the evolving regulatory landscape. Strengthening identity security in IoT networks ensures that organizations can protect sensitive data, maintain regulatory compliance, and build trust in connected environments.

Identity Security for Edge AI and Machine Learning Systems

The convergence of edge computing and artificial intelligence (AI) has revolutionized data processing, enabling real-time decision-making and reducing reliance on centralized cloud infrastructure. Edge AI and machine learning systems operate on distributed networks, processing data locally on devices such as IoT sensors, autonomous vehicles, smart cameras, and industrial control systems. While edge AI enhances efficiency and responsiveness, it also introduces significant identity security challenges. Ensuring that AI models, edge devices, and data streams maintain strong identity authentication and access control is critical to preventing unauthorized manipulation, data breaches, and adversarial attacks.

One of the main identity security risks in edge AI systems is unauthorized access to AI models and data pipelines. Traditional identity and access management (IAM) solutions are often designed for centralized environments, making them difficult to scale across decentralized edge networks. AI models deployed on edge devices must be protected against unauthorized access to prevent model inversion attacks, where attackers attempt to reconstruct training data from AI outputs. Strong authentication mechanisms, such as digital certificates and hardware security modules (HSMs), ensure that only verified entities can access AI models, preventing identity spoofing and unauthorized data manipulation.

Mutual authentication between edge AI devices and cloud services is essential for maintaining secure identity verification. When an edge AI system sends a request to an analytics platform or centralized AI repository, both the sender and recipient must verify each other's identities before exchanging data. Transport Layer Security (TLS) and mutual TLS (mTLS) protocols provide secure identity authentication, ensuring that only authorized AI models and edge devices participate in decision-making processes. Without proper identity authentication, attackers could intercept or manipulate AI training data, leading to biased or incorrect model predictions.

Edge AI identity security must also address model integrity verification. Machine learning models deployed on edge devices are vulnerable to adversarial attacks, where malicious actors manipulate input data to deceive AI systems. Attackers may attempt to impersonate legitimate AI models by injecting compromised identity credentials, leading to biased decision-making or security breaches. Implementing cryptographic hash functions and digital signatures allows organizations to verify the integrity of AI models before deployment, ensuring that only authenticated models are used for edge inference and decision-making.

Access control policies in edge AI environments must be dynamic and context-aware, adjusting permissions based on real-time security conditions. Role-Based Access Control (RBAC) ensures that AI models and edge devices only have access to the data and resources necessary for their functions. Attribute-Based Access Control (ABAC) enhances security by incorporating real-time identity attributes, such as device location, network security posture, and behavioral patterns, into authentication decisions. If an edge AI device attempts to access restricted machine learning models from an untrusted network, ABAC policies can automatically deny access or require additional authentication.

Decentralized identity frameworks provide an innovative approach to securing identity authentication in edge AI environments. Traditional identity management models rely on centralized identity providers, creating potential single points of failure in distributed AI networks. Blockchain-based identity security eliminates these risks by storing AI model identities and authentication records on an immutable distributed ledger. By using decentralized identifiers (DIDs), AI models and edge devices can authenticate securely without relying on external identity providers, reducing the risk of identity fraud and unauthorized access. Smart contracts further enhance security by automating identity validation and enforcing access control policies across distributed AI environments.

AI-driven identity analytics strengthen edge AI security by continuously monitoring authentication patterns and detecting identity-related anomalies. Machine learning algorithms analyze access logs, user behaviors, and device interactions to identify suspicious activity, such as repeated failed authentication attempts or unauthorized access requests. AI-powered identity governance systems can dynamically adjust authentication requirements based on real-time risk assessments, enforcing multi-factor authentication (MFA) for high-risk interactions while allowing seamless authentication for trusted entities. By integrating AI-driven identity security, edge AI environments can proactively detect and mitigate identity threats before they compromise machine learning systems.

Identity federation enhances interoperability in edge AI ecosystems by enabling secure authentication across multiple AI platforms and service providers. Federated identity management allows AI models and edge devices to authenticate once and access multiple machine learning services using a single set of identity credentials. Standards such as OAuth, OpenID Connect, and Security Assertion Markup Language (SAML) facilitate federated authentication, reducing identity management complexity while maintaining strong security. However, federated identity models must ensure that authentication logs and identity metadata do not expose sensitive AI model information to unauthorized parties.

Secure identity lifecycle management ensures that AI models and edge devices maintain strong authentication throughout their operational lifespan. AI model identities must be securely provisioned, updated, and revoked as needed to prevent long-term exposure to security risks. Automated identity credential renewal policies ensure that edge AI models do not continue using outdated authentication methods, reducing the risk of identity compromise. When an AI model is retired or replaced, its identity credentials must be securely revoked to prevent attackers from using obsolete models for adversarial attacks. Identity lifecycle management reduces security risks by ensuring that only actively authenticated AI models operate within edge environments.

Regulatory compliance is a crucial consideration in edge AI identity security, as organizations must adhere to data protection laws and AI governance frameworks. Regulations such as the European Union's AI Act, the General Data Protection Regulation (GDPR), and the National Institute of Standards and Technology (NIST) AI Risk Management Framework impose strict requirements on AI authentication, data privacy, and model transparency. Organizations deploying edge AI solutions must implement identity security policies that align with these regulations, ensuring that AI models and edge devices comply with global security standards. Compliance reporting tools provide visibility into identity authentication events, enabling organizations to demonstrate adherence to regulatory frameworks while maintaining strong AI security.

Quantum-safe identity authentication is becoming increasingly important in securing edge AI systems. Advances in quantum computing could potentially break traditional cryptographic authentication methods, compromising the identity security of AI models and machine learning systems. Post-quantum cryptographic algorithms provide a long-term security solution by ensuring that AI authentication remains resilient against quantum decryption attacks. Lattice-based encryption, hash-based signatures, and quantum-resistant key exchange protocols enhance the security of edge AI identity management, protecting authentication processes from future cyber threats. Organizations must begin transitioning to quantum-safe identity security to maintain trust in AI authentication and protect against evolving quantum risks.

The future of identity security for edge AI and machine learning systems will be shaped by advancements in decentralized authentication, AI-driven identity monitoring, and post-quantum cryptographic techniques. Organizations must implement robust authentication mechanisms, dynamic access control policies, and continuous identity monitoring to prevent adversarial attacks and unauthorized AI manipulation. By leveraging blockchain-based identity security, federated authentication, and AI-powered governance, edge AI ecosystems can achieve strong identity protection while enabling secure and efficient machine learning operations. Strengthening identity security in edge AI environments ensures that AI models remain trustworthy, resilient, and compliant with emerging security regulations.

Identity-Based Zero Touch Provisioning in IoT

Zero Touch Provisioning (ZTP) has emerged as a fundamental approach to managing the onboarding and authentication of IoT devices at scale. With the rapid expansion of IoT ecosystems across industries such as smart cities, healthcare, manufacturing, and logistics, organizations require automated, secure, and efficient methods to deploy devices without manual configuration. Identity-based ZTP ensures that every device is authenticated before joining the network, preventing unauthorized access, identity spoofing, and security breaches. By integrating strong identity verification mechanisms, cryptographic authentication, and policy-driven provisioning workflows, identity-based ZTP enhances IoT security while reducing operational complexity.

One of the biggest challenges in IoT deployment is the secure provisioning of devices in large-scale environments. Traditional provisioning methods require manual configuration, which introduces inefficiencies, human errors, and security vulnerabilities. Static credentials, hardcoded authentication keys, and pre-shared secrets create attack vectors that adversaries can exploit to gain unauthorized access to IoT networks. Identity-based ZTP eliminates these risks by automating the authentication process and ensuring that each device establishes a trusted identity before it is granted network access.

Public Key Infrastructure (PKI) plays a crucial role in identity-based ZTP by enabling cryptographic authentication for IoT devices. When a new device is deployed, it generates a unique cryptographic key pair and requests a digital certificate from a trusted Certificate Authority (CA). This certificate serves as the device's verifiable identity, allowing it to authenticate securely with network controllers, cloud platforms, and other IoT devices. By using certificate-based authentication, organizations eliminate the need for static credentials, reducing the risk of credential-based attacks while ensuring that only authorized devices can participate in the IoT network.

Mutual authentication enhances security in identity-based ZTP by ensuring that both the IoT device and the provisioning system verify each other's identities before establishing communication. This prevents rogue devices from impersonating legitimate IoT assets and prevents unauthorized provisioning attempts. Mutual TLS (mTLS) and cryptographic handshake protocols establish a secure channel between the provisioning server and the device, ensuring that identity validation occurs before any configuration data or credentials are transmitted. This process significantly reduces the risk of man-in-the-middle (MITM) attacks, identity spoofing, and unauthorized device enrollment.

Device identity binding ensures that each IoT device maintains a unique, tamper-proof identity throughout its lifecycle. When a device is manufactured, it can be preloaded with a secure identity key that is cryptographically bound to its hardware. This identity is immutable and serves as the foundation for secure authentication when the device is onboarded into an IoT ecosystem. Hardware Security Modules (HSMs) and Trusted Platform Modules (TPMs) provide tamper-resistant storage for device identity credentials, ensuring that private keys and digital certificates cannot be extracted or manipulated by attackers.

Decentralized identity frameworks offer an alternative approach to traditional centralized provisioning methods by eliminating reliance on a single identity provider. Blockchain-based identity management allows IoT devices to register their identities on a distributed ledger, ensuring that authentication records remain transparent, tamper-proof, and verifiable. Smart contracts automate identity verification during the provisioning process, allowing devices to self-authenticate without requiring manual intervention. By decentralizing identity management, organizations can improve security, reduce the risk of identity fraud, and ensure interoperability across different IoT service providers.

Zero Trust security principles align with identity-based ZTP by enforcing continuous authentication and verification for IoT devices. In a Zero Trust model, no device is automatically trusted based on its network location or initial provisioning status. Instead, each device must continuously prove its identity before accessing critical resources. Identity-based ZTP incorporates dynamic access control policies that evaluate real-time security conditions before granting provisioning requests. If a device exhibits suspicious behavior during onboarding, such as connecting from an untrusted network or failing multiple authentication attempts, the provisioning system can automatically reject its request or enforce additional security measures.

AI-driven identity threat detection strengthens security during the ZTP process by analyzing authentication patterns and detecting anomalies in real time. Machine learning models monitor device behavior, provisioning requests, and network interactions to identify potential identity-based attacks. If an AI-driven security platform detects unusual authentication attempts, such as multiple failed provisioning requests or identity tampering attempts, it can trigger automated security responses. These responses may include flagging the device for manual review, revoking provisioning credentials, or isolating suspicious devices from the network. By integrating AI-driven identity analytics, organizations can enhance ZTP security while reducing the risk of identity compromise.

Federated identity management simplifies ZTP for IoT ecosystems that span multiple organizations, cloud platforms, and service providers. Federated authentication allows IoT devices to provision securely across different networks using a common identity framework. Standards such as OAuth, OpenID Connect, and Security Assertion Markup Language (SAML) enable seamless identity verification across distributed environments, ensuring that devices can authenticate once and access multiple services without requiring separate credentials. Federated identity models improve interoperability while maintaining strong authentication and access control policies.

Identity lifecycle management ensures that IoT devices maintain secure authentication throughout their operational lifespan. Identity-based ZTP incorporates automated credential rotation, key renewal, and certificate revocation policies to prevent identity compromise. When a device reaches the end of its lifecycle, secure decommissioning processes revoke its identity credentials, ensuring that it cannot be exploited by attackers. Automated identity lifecycle management reduces administrative overhead while maintaining the integrity of IoT identity authentication.

Regulatory compliance plays a key role in shaping identity-based ZTP policies for IoT security. Data protection laws such as the General Data Protection Regulation (GDPR), the California Consumer Privacy Act (CCPA), and the NIST Cybersecurity Framework impose strict authentication, encryption, and access control requirements for IoT devices. Identity-based ZTP ensures compliance by implementing strong authentication mechanisms, securing provisioning workflows, and enforcing data sovereignty policies. Organizations deploying IoT solutions must align their identity provisioning strategies with regulatory requirements to avoid compliance violations while maintaining secure identity authentication.

Quantum-safe identity authentication is an emerging consideration for identity-based ZTP, as quantum computing advancements could render traditional cryptographic techniques vulnerable to decryption. Post-quantum cryptographic algorithms provide long-term security by ensuring that IoT authentication mechanisms remain resistant to quantum attacks. Lattice-based encryption, hash-based signatures, and quantum-resistant key exchange protocols enhance identity-based ZTP by protecting provisioning workflows from future cryptographic threats. Organizations must begin transitioning to quantum-safe identity authentication to ensure the continued security of IoT provisioning processes.

The future of identity-based ZTP will be shaped by advancements in AI-driven identity analytics, blockchain-based authentication, and post-quantum cryptographic techniques. Organizations must implement robust authentication mechanisms, enforce continuous identity verification, and integrate automated security policies to protect IoT devices from unauthorized provisioning attempts. By leveraging Zero Trust security models, federated identity frameworks, and decentralized authentication methods, identity-based ZTP enables scalable, secure, and compliant IoT deployments. Strengthening identity security in ZTP ensures that IoT ecosystems remain resilient against evolving cyber threats while enabling seamless device onboarding and authentication.

Case Studies: Identity Security Breaches in IoT

The widespread adoption of IoT devices across industries has introduced significant security risks, particularly concerning identity authentication and access control. Numerous high-profile security breaches have demonstrated the vulnerabilities of IoT identity management, exposing organizations to data theft, operational disruptions, and large-scale cyberattacks. Examining real-world identity security breaches in IoT provides valuable insights into the weaknesses in current authentication mechanisms and highlights the importance of robust identity security frameworks.

One of the most notorious IoT identity security breaches occurred in 2016 when the Mirai botnet exploited weak authentication mechanisms to compromise thousands of IoT devices worldwide. The attackers used a list of commonly used default credentials to gain unauthorized access to vulnerable IoT devices, including IP cameras, routers, and digital video recorders. Once infected, these devices were transformed into a massive botnet that launched one of the largest distributed denial-of-service (DDoS) attacks in history. The attack targeted major internet infrastructure providers, disrupting services for millions of users across multiple industries. The Mirai attack demonstrated the dangers of weak identity security in IoT, emphasizing the need for strong authentication practices, mandatory password changes, and continuous identity monitoring to prevent credential-based attacks.

Another significant identity security breach in IoT involved a large-scale attack on a connected healthcare system. In this incident, attackers exploited weak authentication controls in medical IoT devices, such as smart infusion pumps and patient monitoring systems. The compromised devices were used to gain unauthorized access to hospital networks, allowing attackers to exfiltrate patient records and manipulate medical data. The breach not only violated patient privacy regulations, such as the Health Insurance Portability and Accountability Act (HIPAA), but also posed life-threatening risks by altering critical treatment protocols. The attack underscored the importance of enforcing multi-factor authentication (MFA), implementing strict role-based access control (RBAC) policies, and continuously monitoring identity authentication events in medical IoT environments.

In the industrial sector, an IoT identity breach affected a smart manufacturing facility, where attackers leveraged stolen credentials to gain access to connected industrial control systems (ICS). The attackers manipulated identity authentication logs to bypass security measures, allowing them to remotely control programmable logic controllers (PLCs) and other critical manufacturing equipment. This breach resulted in production delays, unauthorized modifications to manufacturing processes, and significant financial losses. Investigations revealed that the facility relied on static credentials without proper identity lifecycle management, making it easier for attackers to exploit outdated authentication mechanisms. Implementing cryptographic identity authentication, certificate-based authentication, and identity lifecycle automation would have significantly reduced the risk of unauthorized access in this scenario.

The transportation sector has also experienced IoT identity security breaches, with connected vehicles being targeted through weak identity authentication protocols. In one case, attackers successfully exploited identity vulnerabilities in a vehicle-to-everything (V2X) communication system, allowing them to impersonate legitimate vehicles and send false traffic signals. This breach created dangerous road conditions by transmitting fake collision alerts, causing unnecessary braking and traffic disruptions. The attackers leveraged identity spoofing techniques to impersonate trusted vehicle identities, bypassing authentication mechanisms. Strengthening identity authentication through public key infrastructure (PKI), certificate-based authentication, and cryptographic signatures would have mitigated the risks associated with identity spoofing in V2X networks.

Retail organizations using IoT-enabled point-of-sale (POS) systems have also been victims of identity security breaches. In a notable case, attackers infiltrated a retail IoT network by exploiting a weakly protected smart payment terminal. The attackers used stolen identity credentials to gain unauthorized access to the network, allowing them to intercept customer payment data and execute fraudulent transactions. The breach resulted in financial losses, reputational damage, and legal consequences for the affected organization. The attack highlighted the need for federated identity management, encrypted identity authentication, and continuous monitoring of IoT authentication events to detect and prevent unauthorized access.

Another major identity security breach occurred in smart home IoT devices, where attackers exploited cloud-based identity authentication weaknesses to gain control of connected security cameras and smart locks. Homeowners reported cases of unauthorized access to their surveillance systems, with attackers live-streaming security footage and even issuing voice commands through compromised smart assistants. The breach exposed vulnerabilities in cloud-based identity authentication, demonstrating the risks associated with weak password policies, lack of multi-factor authentication, and insufficient encryption of identity credentials. Strengthening identity security through decentralized identity frameworks, biometric authentication, and AI-driven anomaly detection would have provided better protection against unauthorized access.

In a case involving IoT identity fraud, attackers compromised an energy grid's smart meter authentication system, allowing them to manipulate billing data and gain unauthorized access to energy distribution controls. The attackers exploited identity authentication weaknesses in smart meters, forging authentication credentials to override legitimate billing records. This breach not only resulted in financial losses but also raised concerns about the security of critical infrastructure. Deploying blockchain-based identity authentication, attribute-based access control (ABAC), and quantum-safe cryptographic authentication would have enhanced identity security and prevented unauthorized modifications to smart meter data.

The growing reliance on IoT in the financial sector has also led to identity security breaches involving connected ATMs and banking IoT devices. In one case, cybercriminals exploited weak identity authentication in IoT-enabled banking kiosks, allowing them to bypass transaction verification processes. The attackers used cloned authentication credentials to withdraw funds and access customer banking information. The breach exposed vulnerabilities in IoT identity authentication, emphasizing the need for hardware-based security modules (HSMs), biometric authentication, and AI-powered identity monitoring to detect fraudulent authentication attempts.

An IoT identity security breach in a smart city deployment demonstrated the risks of weak authentication in public infrastructure. Attackers gained unauthorized access to connected traffic lights and public surveillance systems by exploiting identity authentication weaknesses in IoT control units. The breach allowed attackers to manipulate traffic signals, creating road congestion and potential safety hazards. The incident highlighted the need for decentralized identity authentication, certificate-based mutual authentication, and continuous AI-driven identity monitoring to prevent unauthorized access to critical smart city infrastructure.

Each of these case studies demonstrates the severe consequences of IoT identity security breaches across different industries. The reliance on weak authentication mechanisms, lack of identity monitoring, and failure to implement cryptographic authentication have contributed to large-scale cyberattacks, financial losses, and compromised public safety. Strengthening identity security in IoT requires a combination of multi-factor authentication, AI-driven threat detection, federated identity management, and continuous identity verification. By learning from these breaches and implementing robust identity security frameworks, organizations can mitigate risks, protect sensitive data, and ensure the integrity of IoT ecosystems.

Best Practices for IoT Identity Risk Management

The rapid expansion of IoT ecosystems has introduced complex identity management challenges that require robust risk mitigation strategies. As billions of devices connect to networks, organizations must ensure that identity authentication, authorization, and lifecycle management are effectively secured to prevent unauthorized access, data breaches, and cyber threats. IoT identity risk management involves implementing strong authentication mechanisms, continuous monitoring, and proactive security controls to protect device identities from compromise. By adopting best practices in IoT identity risk management, organizations can reduce vulnerabilities, enforce compliance, and enhance the overall security posture of connected environments.

One of the fundamental aspects of IoT identity risk management is implementing strong authentication mechanisms to verify device identities before granting access to network resources. Weak authentication, such as static passwords, default credentials, and pre-shared keys, exposes IoT networks to identity-based attacks. Public Key Infrastructure (PKI) provides a scalable authentication solution by issuing digital certificates to devices, ensuring that each device has a unique and verifiable identity. Certificate-based authentication eliminates the need for password-based credentials, reducing the risk of credential theft, brute-force attacks, and identity spoofing. Organizations should enforce mutual authentication, where both the IoT device and the network authenticate each other using cryptographic protocols such as Transport Layer Security (TLS) and mutual TLS (mTLS).

Multi-factor authentication (MFA) strengthens IoT identity security by requiring multiple identity verification factors before granting access. Traditional username-password authentication is inadequate for IoT environments, where devices and applications often operate autonomously. MFA combines factors such as biometric authentication, hardware tokens, and cryptographic signatures to ensure that only legitimate entities can access IoT systems. By enforcing MFA at the device, network, and cloud levels, organizations can reduce the likelihood of unauthorized access and identity compromise.

Continuous identity monitoring is essential for detecting and responding to identity-related threats in real time. AI-driven security analytics analyze authentication logs, device behaviors, and access requests to identify anomalies that may indicate an identity compromise. Machine learning models detect patterns of suspicious activity, such as repeated failed authentication attempts, identity spoofing attempts, and unusual access locations. When an anomaly is detected, automated security responses can be triggered, including revoking credentials, enforcing additional authentication steps, or isolating suspicious devices from the network. AI-driven identity risk management enables organizations to respond proactively to emerging threats, reducing the impact of identity-based attacks.

Implementing Zero Trust security principles enhances IoT identity risk management by enforcing continuous authentication and verification. Traditional network security models assume that devices inside the network perimeter can be trusted, creating security gaps that attackers exploit. In a Zero Trust model, no device or user is automatically trusted based on location or prior authentication. Instead, each access request is verified based on real-time identity attributes, contextual data, and risk assessments. Zero Trust identity security ensures that only authenticated and authorized devices can access IoT resources, reducing the risk of lateral movement attacks and unauthorized data access.

Role-Based Access Control (RBAC) and Attribute-Based Access Control (ABAC) provide structured identity risk management by ensuring that IoT devices and users only have access to the resources necessary for their functions. RBAC assigns permissions based on predefined roles, limiting the exposure of sensitive data and systems. ABAC extends this approach by incorporating real-time attributes such as device location, security posture, and operational status into access control decisions. Dynamic access management policies prevent unauthorized access by adjusting identity permissions based on contextual risk factors.

Decentralized identity frameworks enhance IoT identity security by eliminating reliance on centralized identity providers, reducing the risk of single points of failure. Blockchain-based identity management allows IoT devices to authenticate securely using distributed ledgers, ensuring that identity credentials remain tamper-proof and verifiable. Decentralized identifiers (DIDs) provide self-sovereign identity management, allowing devices to control their authentication credentials without relying on third-party identity authorities. Smart contracts automate identity verification and access control, improving the efficiency and security of identity risk management.

Secure identity provisioning ensures that IoT devices receive authenticated credentials before being deployed into networks. Zero Touch Provisioning (ZTP) automates secure device onboarding by enabling IoT devices to self-authenticate using cryptographic identity verification. ZTP eliminates the need for manual configuration, reducing human errors and security misconfigurations. Identity binding techniques, such as embedding cryptographic identity keys during device manufacturing, ensure that only verified devices can enroll in IoT networks.

Identity lifecycle management plays a critical role in mitigating IoT identity risks by ensuring that identity credentials remain secure throughout their operational lifespan. Organizations must implement automated processes for credential rotation, key renewal, and access revocation to prevent long-term exposure to identity compromise. When an IoT device is retired or decommissioned, its identity credentials must be securely revoked to prevent unauthorized reuse. Identity lifecycle automation reduces administrative overhead while ensuring that only active and authenticated devices maintain network access.

Regulatory compliance is a key factor in IoT identity risk management, as organizations must align their identity authentication policies with data protection and cybersecurity regulations. Compliance frameworks such as the General Data Protection Regulation (GDPR), the National Institute of Standards and Technology (NIST) Cybersecurity Framework, and the California Consumer Privacy Act (CCPA) impose strict identity authentication, encryption, and access control requirements. Organizations must enforce regulatory-compliant identity security measures, including encryption of identity credentials, logging of authentication events, and user consent mechanisms. Compliance reporting tools enable organizations to track identity access patterns, generate audit logs, and demonstrate adherence to security standards.

Threat intelligence integration enhances IoT identity risk management by providing real-time insights into evolving identity-based cyber threats. By analyzing global threat intelligence feeds, organizations can identify known attack vectors, such as credential stuffing, identity spoofing, and brute-force authentication attempts. AI-powered security platforms correlate threat intelligence with identity authentication events, enabling organizations to detect and mitigate emerging threats before they impact IoT systems. Automated identity risk mitigation strategies include blocking suspicious authentication requests, enforcing additional verification steps for high-risk devices, and dynamically adjusting access policies based on threat intelligence data.

Quantum-safe identity security is becoming increasingly important as quantum computing threatens traditional cryptographic authentication mechanisms. Post-quantum cryptographic algorithms provide long-term protection for IoT identity authentication, ensuring that encryption keys and digital signatures remain resistant to quantum decryption attacks. Organizations must begin transitioning to quantum-resistant identity security solutions to safeguard IoT authentication processes from future cryptographic vulnerabilities.

By implementing a combination of strong authentication mechanisms, continuous monitoring, Zero Trust security principles, and regulatory compliance enforcement, organizations can effectively manage IoT identity risks. The evolving landscape of IoT security requires adaptive identity risk management strategies that integrate AI-driven security analytics, blockchain-based authentication, and post-quantum cryptographic techniques. Strengthening identity security in IoT environments ensures that organizations can mitigate risks, prevent unauthorized access, and protect sensitive data while maintaining the integrity and reliability of connected devices.

The Convergence of IoT, Edge, and Identity Security

The rapid expansion of the Internet of Things (IoT) and edge computing has introduced new security challenges, particularly in the area of identity authentication and access control. As more devices connect to networks and process data at the edge, traditional security models that rely on centralized identity management systems struggle to keep up with the scale, complexity, and dynamic nature of these environments. The convergence of IoT, edge computing, and identity security requires a holistic approach that integrates strong authentication, continuous identity verification, and adaptive access control mechanisms. Ensuring that IoT devices, edge nodes, and users can securely authenticate and interact within distributed networks is critical for maintaining data integrity, preventing unauthorized access, and mitigating cyber threats.

One of the key factors driving the convergence of IoT and edge computing is the need for real-time data processing. Unlike traditional cloud-centric models, where data is transmitted to centralized servers for processing, edge computing enables devices to analyze and act on data locally. This reduces latency, improves efficiency, and enhances decision-making capabilities in critical applications such as autonomous vehicles, smart cities, industrial automation, and healthcare. However, the decentralization of data processing also increases security risks, as IoT devices and edge nodes operate outside traditional security perimeters. Identity security ensures that only authenticated devices and authorized users can access edge computing resources, preventing identity spoofing, unauthorized access, and data manipulation.

Strong authentication mechanisms are essential for securing identity interactions in IoT and edge environments. Traditional password-based authentication is insufficient for IoT devices, which often operate autonomously and lack user interfaces. Instead, certificate-based authentication, cryptographic key exchanges, and biometric identity verification provide more secure alternatives. Public Key Infrastructure (PKI) enables IoT devices and edge nodes to authenticate using digital certificates, ensuring that only trusted entities can participate in network communications. Mutual authentication further strengthens security by requiring both devices and edge servers to verify each other's identities before exchanging data. By implementing cryptographic authentication, organizations can prevent identity-based attacks and ensure that data remains protected at the edge.

Zero Trust security principles play a crucial role in the convergence of IoT, edge, and identity security. In a Zero Trust model, no device, user, or application is automatically trusted based on its location or previous authentication status. Instead, continuous identity verification is enforced at every access request, requiring devices and users to authenticate dynamically based on contextual risk factors. Attribute-Based Access Control (ABAC) enhances Zero Trust by evaluating real-time identity attributes, such as device health, location, network security posture, and behavioral analytics, before granting access to edge computing resources. This dynamic approach ensures that only trusted devices and users can access sensitive data, reducing the risk of identity compromise.

Decentralized identity frameworks provide a scalable solution for managing identity security in distributed IoT and edge computing environments. Traditional identity management models rely on centralized authentication servers, creating potential single points of failure and scalability challenges. Blockchain-based identity security eliminates these risks by storing identity credentials on a distributed ledger, ensuring that authentication records remain tamper-proof and verifiable. Decentralized Identifiers (DIDs) enable IoT devices to manage their own authentication credentials, reducing reliance on third-party identity providers and enhancing privacy. Smart contracts automate identity verification processes, allowing edge devices to authenticate securely without requiring direct interaction with central authentication servers. The adoption of decentralized identity frameworks strengthens security while improving interoperability across different IoT and edge computing platforms.

AI-driven identity security enhances the protection of IoT and edge environments by continuously monitoring authentication events and detecting anomalies in real time. Machine learning algorithms analyze access logs, user behaviors, and device interactions to identify potential identity threats, such as unauthorized access attempts, credential abuse, and identity spoofing. AI-powered security platforms can dynamically adjust authentication policies based on detected risks, enforcing additional verification steps for high-risk devices while allowing seamless authentication for trusted entities. By integrating AI-driven identity monitoring, organizations can proactively detect and mitigate identity-related cyber threats before they compromise IoT and edge networks.

Federated identity management improves interoperability across IoT and edge ecosystems by enabling seamless authentication across multiple platforms, service providers, and network domains. Federated identity frameworks allow devices, users, and applications to authenticate once and access multiple edge computing environments without requiring separate credentials for each system. Standards such as OAuth, OpenID Connect, and Security Assertion Markup Language (SAML) facilitate secure identity federation while ensuring compliance with access control policies. Federated authentication reduces identity management complexity and enhances security by enforcing consistent authentication policies across distributed IoT and edge networks.

Identity lifecycle management ensures that authentication credentials remain secure throughout the operational lifespan of IoT devices and edge nodes. Automated identity provisioning allows new devices to be securely onboarded into networks without requiring manual configuration. Secure identity binding techniques, such as embedding cryptographic identity keys during device manufacturing, ensure that only verified devices can enroll in edge computing environments. Continuous identity credential updates, key rotations, and certificate renewals prevent long-term exposure to security vulnerabilities. When a device reaches end-of-life, its identity credentials must be revoked to prevent unauthorized reuse. Automated identity lifecycle management reduces administrative overhead while maintaining strong authentication security across IoT and edge deployments.

Regulatory compliance is a critical consideration in the convergence of IoT, edge, and identity security. Data protection laws such as the General Data Protection Regulation (GDPR), the California Consumer Privacy Act (CCPA), and the National Institute of Standards and Technology (NIST) cybersecurity guidelines impose strict authentication, encryption, and access control requirements for connected environments. Organizations must implement regulatory-compliant identity security policies, ensuring that authentication processes align with industry standards while protecting sensitive data. Secure logging, audit trails, and real-time access monitoring enable organizations to demonstrate compliance while maintaining strong identity governance.

Quantum-safe identity security is becoming increasingly important as quantum computing advancements threaten traditional cryptographic authentication mechanisms. Post-quantum cryptographic algorithms provide long-term protection for IoT and edge identity authentication, ensuring that encryption keys, digital signatures, and access control mechanisms remain resistant to quantum decryption attacks.

Organizations must begin transitioning to quantum-resistant identity authentication methods to future-proof IoT and edge security frameworks.

The convergence of IoT, edge, and identity security requires a multi-layered approach that integrates cryptographic authentication, Zero Trust security models, decentralized identity frameworks, AI-driven threat detection, and compliance enforcement. Organizations must adopt identity security strategies that address the unique challenges of distributed environments while ensuring seamless authentication and access control across IoT and edge networks. By leveraging advanced identity security solutions, organizations can mitigate risks, enhance trust, and maintain the integrity of connected ecosystems in an era of rapid digital transformation.

Future Trends and Innovations in Identity Security for IoT

The rapid evolution of IoT ecosystems has created a growing need for advanced identity security solutions that can address the increasing scale, complexity, and cyber threats associated with connected devices. As IoT networks expand across industries, including smart cities, healthcare, industrial automation, and transportation, identity security must evolve to ensure robust authentication, access control, and data protection. Future trends and innovations in IoT identity security will focus on improving authentication mechanisms, enhancing privacy, integrating artificial intelligence, adopting decentralized identity frameworks, and preparing for the challenges of quantum computing.

One of the most significant trends in IoT identity security is the shift towards passwordless authentication. Traditional password-based authentication methods are no longer viable for large-scale IoT deployments due to their vulnerability to credential theft, brute-force attacks, and identity spoofing. Instead, organizations are adopting passwordless authentication mechanisms that leverage biometrics, cryptographic keys, and hardware-based authentication. Biometric authentication, such as facial recognition, fingerprint scanning, and voice verification, ensures that only authorized users and devices can access IoT networks. Cryptographic authentication methods, such as public key infrastructure (PKI) and hardware security modules (HSMs), eliminate the need for static credentials by using digital certificates and cryptographic signatures to verify device identities.

Decentralized identity management is emerging as a revolutionary approach to securing IoT authentication. Traditional identity management systems rely on centralized databases and identity providers, creating single points of failure and increasing the risk of identity theft. Decentralized identity frameworks, based on blockchain technology, enable IoT devices to manage their own authentication credentials without relying on third-party identity authorities. Decentralized Identifiers (DIDs) provide self-sovereign identity management, allowing IoT devices to authenticate securely while maintaining privacy and control over identity data. Blockchain-based identity authentication ensures that identity records remain tamper-proof, verifiable, and resistant to unauthorized modifications.

The integration of artificial intelligence and machine learning in identity security is transforming the way IoT networks detect and respond to identity-based threats. AI-driven identity analytics continuously monitor authentication patterns, device behaviors, and access requests to identify anomalies that may indicate unauthorized access or identity compromise. Machine learning models analyze historical authentication data to detect deviations from normal behavior, such as unusual access locations, repeated failed login attempts, or identity spoofing attempts. When a threat is detected, AI-powered security platforms can enforce adaptive authentication policies, requiring additional verification steps for high-risk interactions while allowing seamless authentication for trusted entities. The combination of AI-driven threat detection and dynamic authentication ensures that IoT identity security remains proactive and resilient against evolving cyber threats.

Zero Trust security models are gaining traction in IoT identity management, replacing traditional perimeter-based security approaches. In a Zero Trust model, no device, user, or application is automatically trusted based on its location or previous authentication status. Instead, continuous identity verification is enforced at every access request, ensuring that devices must prove their identity dynamically based on contextual risk factors. Attribute-Based Access Control (ABAC) enhances Zero Trust by evaluating real-time identity attributes, such as device health, location, and security posture, before granting access to IoT resources. The adoption of Zero Trust identity security reduces the risk of unauthorized access, insider threats, and lateral movement attacks in IoT networks.

Federated identity management is becoming a critical component of IoT security, enabling seamless authentication across multiple platforms, service providers, and network domains. Federated identity frameworks allow IoT devices, users, and applications to authenticate once and securely access multiple services without requiring separate credentials for each system. Standards such as OAuth, OpenID Connect, and Security Assertion Markup Language (SAML) facilitate federated authentication while ensuring compliance with access control policies. Federated identity management enhances interoperability, reduces identity management complexity, and strengthens security by enforcing consistent authentication policies across distributed IoT ecosystems.

Quantum-safe identity security is a growing area of focus as quantum computing threatens traditional cryptographic authentication mechanisms. Current encryption algorithms, including RSA and ECC, are vulnerable to quantum decryption techniques, potentially compromising identity authentication processes. Post-quantum cryptographic algorithms provide a long-term security solution by ensuring that encryption keys, digital signatures, and authentication protocols remain resistant to quantum attacks. Lattice-based encryption, hash-based signatures, and quantum-resistant key exchange protocols are being developed to enhance IoT identity authentication. Organizations must begin transitioning to quantum-safe identity security to future-proof authentication mechanisms against emerging quantum computing threats.

Edge computing is playing a larger role in IoT identity security, enabling real-time authentication and data processing at the network edge. Traditional cloud-based authentication models introduce latency and scalability challenges, making them impractical for high-speed IoT applications such as autonomous vehicles, industrial automation, and smart grids. Edge-based identity security ensures that authentication decisions are made closer to the devices, reducing response times and improving security resilience. AI-powered edge identity security enables decentralized authentication, allowing IoT devices to verify identities locally without relying on central identity providers. By integrating identity authentication at the edge, organizations can enhance security, minimize latency, and improve operational efficiency.

The adoption of identity-based zero-touch provisioning (ZTP) is streamlining IoT device onboarding and authentication. Traditional provisioning methods require manual configuration, increasing security risks and deployment inefficiencies. Identity-based ZTP automates device enrollment by allowing IoT devices to authenticate themselves securely using cryptographic identity verification. Public Key Infrastructure (PKI) and certificate-based authentication enable devices to register with IoT networks automatically while ensuring that only verified entities are granted access. ZTP reduces human intervention, eliminates misconfigurations, and strengthens identity security by ensuring that devices are authenticated before they are operational.

Privacy-enhancing identity security techniques are gaining importance as IoT networks process increasing amounts of sensitive data. Privacy-preserving authentication methods, such as zero-knowledge proofs (ZKPs) and homomorphic encryption, allow IoT devices to authenticate without revealing unnecessary identity details. Zero-knowledge authentication enables devices to prove their identity without transmitting sensitive credentials, reducing the risk of identity exposure and unauthorized tracking. Homomorphic encryption ensures that identity verification processes remain encrypted throughout authentication, protecting identity data from interception and manipulation. These privacy-preserving innovations strengthen identity security while ensuring compliance with data protection regulations.

Regulatory compliance will continue to shape the future of IoT identity security, requiring organizations to implement authentication measures that align with data protection laws and cybersecurity frameworks. Regulations such as the General Data Protection Regulation (GDPR), the California Consumer Privacy Act (CCPA), and the NIST Cybersecurity Framework impose strict requirements on identity authentication, access control, and encryption. IoT organizations must implement regulatory-compliant identity security policies to ensure that authentication processes align with industry standards while protecting sensitive identity data. Compliance-driven identity security frameworks enhance transparency, accountability, and trust in IoT ecosystems.

As IoT identity security evolves, organizations must embrace emerging technologies and security frameworks to mitigate identity-based cyber threats. The adoption of passwordless authentication, decentralized identity management, AI-driven security analytics, Zero Trust identity security, and quantum-resistant cryptographic techniques will play a crucial role in shaping the future of IoT authentication. Strengthening identity security ensures that IoT ecosystems remain resilient, secure, and compliant with evolving cybersecurity challenges, enabling the next generation of connected devices to operate safely and efficiently in an increasingly digital world.

The Road Ahead for IoT and Edge Identity Security

As the Internet of Things (IoT) and edge computing continue to evolve, the need for robust identity security has never been greater. The exponential growth of connected devices, combined with the increasing complexity of distributed networks, presents both opportunities and challenges for security professionals. Identity security is at the core of IoT and edge computing, ensuring that only trusted devices, users, and applications can access and interact within these ecosystems. The road ahead for IoT and edge identity security will be shaped by advances in authentication mechanisms, the adoption of decentralized identity frameworks, the integration of artificial intelligence, and the emergence of quantum-resistant cryptographic techniques.

The future of identity security in IoT and edge computing begins with stronger authentication mechanisms that eliminate traditional vulnerabilities. Password-based authentication has long been the weakest link in security, leading to identity theft, credential stuffing attacks, and unauthorized access. Moving forward, passwordless authentication methods will become the standard for securing IoT identities. Biometric authentication, cryptographic key exchanges, and hardware-backed security modules will replace passwords, ensuring that authentication is both seamless and resistant to compromise. Organizations will need to implement digital certificates, token-based authentication, and multi-factor authentication (MFA) to strengthen identity verification across distributed networks.

Decentralized identity management will play a pivotal role in the future of IoT security, reducing reliance on centralized authentication providers and improving privacy. Traditional identity management models create single points of failure, making them vulnerable to cyberattacks and unauthorized access. Blockchain-based identity frameworks will provide a secure and verifiable way for IoT devices to manage their authentication credentials without exposing sensitive information to third parties. Decentralized Identifiers (DIDs) will enable self-sovereign identity management, allowing devices and users to control their authentication processes while maintaining interoperability across different platforms and service providers. By leveraging blockchain for identity verification, organizations can reduce the risk of identity fraud, enhance transparency, and improve trust in IoT ecosystems.

Artificial intelligence (AI) and machine learning will continue to revolutionize identity security by enabling real-time threat detection and adaptive authentication. AI-driven identity analytics will monitor authentication patterns, device behaviors, and access requests to identify potential security risks before they escalate. Machine learning algorithms will detect anomalies such as unusual login attempts, unauthorized identity spoofing, or behavioral deviations that indicate identity compromise. AI-powered security platforms will enforce risk-based authentication policies, dynamically adjusting authentication requirements based on real-time threat assessments. The integration of AI into identity security will enhance automation, reduce human intervention, and provide a proactive defense against identity-based cyber threats.

The concept of Zero Trust security will become the foundation of IoT and edge identity security, replacing traditional perimeter-based security models. In a Zero Trust environment, every device, user, and application must continuously verify its identity before gaining access to network resources. Trust is never assumed based on location, previous authentication, or device status. Instead, dynamic access control mechanisms will evaluate identity attributes, contextual data, and security posture before granting access. Attribute-Based Access Control (ABAC) will complement Zero Trust by factoring in real-time conditions such as device location, operational behavior, and risk level. Implementing Zero Trust identity security will reduce the risk of insider threats, lateral movement attacks, and unauthorized access to sensitive IoT data.

Federated identity management will continue to shape how IoT and edge devices interact across multiple service providers, cloud platforms, and network domains. As IoT ecosystems grow, devices will need to authenticate seamlessly across different environments without requiring multiple credentials. Federated authentication frameworks, such as OAuth, OpenID Connect, and Security Assertion Markup Language (SAML), will enable devices to authenticate once and gain access to multiple services securely. However, federated identity systems must be designed to protect privacy, ensuring that authentication metadata does not expose sensitive identity information to unauthorized parties. By adopting federated identity models, organizations will streamline authentication, improve interoperability, and enhance user experience while maintaining strong security controls.

Quantum computing presents a significant challenge for IoT identity security, as traditional cryptographic authentication mechanisms will become vulnerable to quantum attacks. RSA, ECC, and other widely used encryption algorithms will no longer provide sufficient security once quantum computers become powerful enough to break them. Organizations must prepare for this transition by adopting quantum-safe identity authentication methods. Post-quantum cryptographic algorithms, such as lattice-based encryption, hash-based signatures, and quantum-resistant key exchange protocols, will ensure that IoT authentication remains secure against future quantum threats. Transitioning to quantum-safe identity security will be a critical step in protecting IoT ecosystems from emerging cyber risks.

Edge computing will continue to shape the future of identity security by enabling real-time authentication and access control at the network edge. Traditional cloud-based authentication models introduce latency and scalability limitations, making them less suitable for time-sensitive IoT applications such as autonomous vehicles, industrial automation, and smart healthcare. Edge-based identity security will allow authentication decisions to be made locally, reducing response times and improving resilience against network failures. AI-driven edge identity security will enable decentralized authentication, allowing IoT devices to verify their identities without relying on centralized identity providers. By integrating identity security at the edge, organizations can enhance scalability, reduce latency, and improve overall security posture.

Zero Touch Provisioning (ZTP) will become the standard for secure IoT device onboarding and authentication. As IoT networks continue to scale, manual device provisioning becomes impractical and introduces security risks. Identity-based ZTP will automate device enrollment, allowing new IoT devices to authenticate and configure themselves securely upon deployment. PKI-based authentication, certificate-based provisioning, and cryptographic identity verification will ensure that only trusted devices can join IoT networks. Automating identity provisioning will enhance security, reduce human error, and enable seamless scalability in IoT deployments.

Regulatory compliance will remain a driving force in shaping IoT identity security policies. As governments and regulatory bodies implement stricter data protection laws, organizations must align their identity authentication practices with global cybersecurity standards. Regulations such as the General Data Protection Regulation (GDPR), the California Consumer Privacy Act (CCPA), and the NIST Cybersecurity Framework will impose mandatory security requirements for IoT identity authentication. Organizations must implement encryption, access control policies, audit logging, and user consent mechanisms to comply with regulatory standards while protecting identity data. Compliance-driven identity security will enhance transparency, accountability, and trust in IoT ecosystems.

As IoT and edge computing ecosystems continue to expand, identity security must evolve to address emerging cyber threats and regulatory requirements. Organizations must embrace advanced authentication mechanisms, decentralized identity frameworks, AI-driven security analytics, Zero Trust security models, and post-quantum cryptographic techniques to safeguard IoT identities. Strengthening identity security will ensure that IoT devices, users, and applications can operate securely, efficiently, and in compliance with global security standards. By prioritizing identity security, organizations will pave the way for a safer, more resilient, and more trustworthy connected world.